MY BIG BOOK OF WORDS AND PICTURES

HINKLER
BOOKS

MY BIG BOOK OF
WORDS
AND PICTURES

Words are fun.
You see and hear them every day.
You can use words to talk.
You can use words to write.
You can read words.

Do you know the names of all the things around you?
Do you know a thousand words?
You can learn them in this book.
Do you know the alphabet?
Do you know what a dictionary is?
You can find out by reading this book.

FIRST 1000 WORDS

FIRST PICTURE DICTIONARY

Has pictures and words for a thousand different things.

Some words are easy and you will already know them.

This is a cat.

Some words are harder, and you might not know them

This is a xylophone.

Have fun learning new words!

A dictionary is a list of words that tells you what each word means.

In this dictionary, there are pictures next to each word, in case you have never heard the word before.

Sometimes, it is good to have a picture to help you understand a word.

Like this:

pumpkin

A **pumpkin** is a large, orange fruit.

First
1000 WORDS

JULIE HAYDON

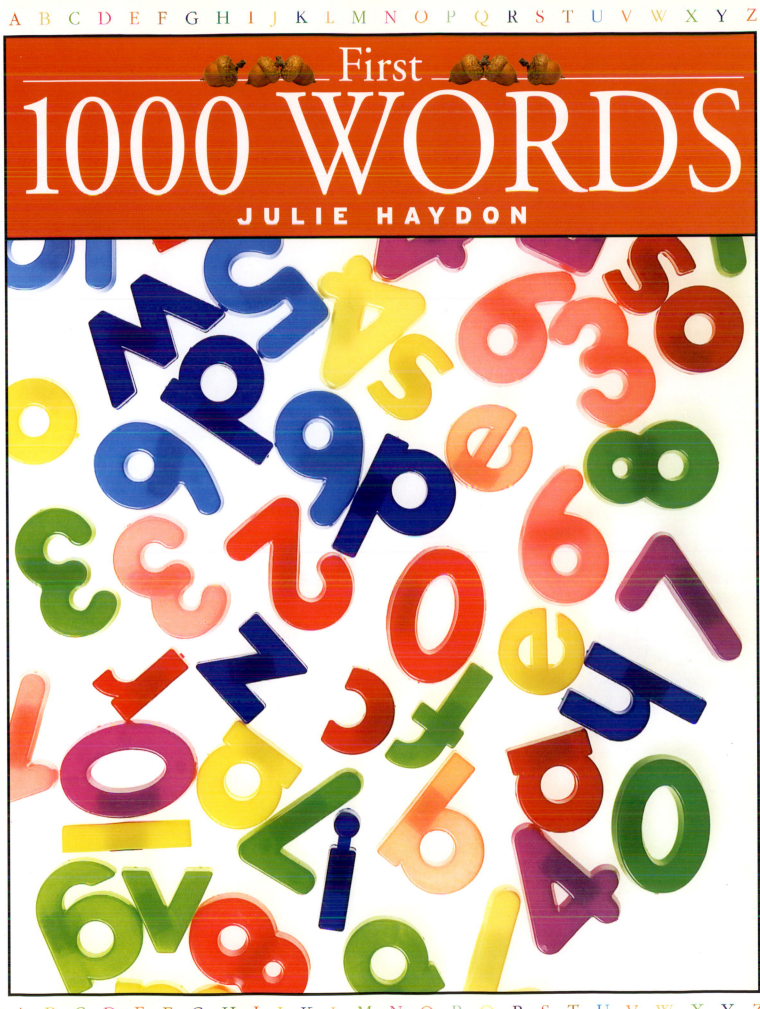

THE Face

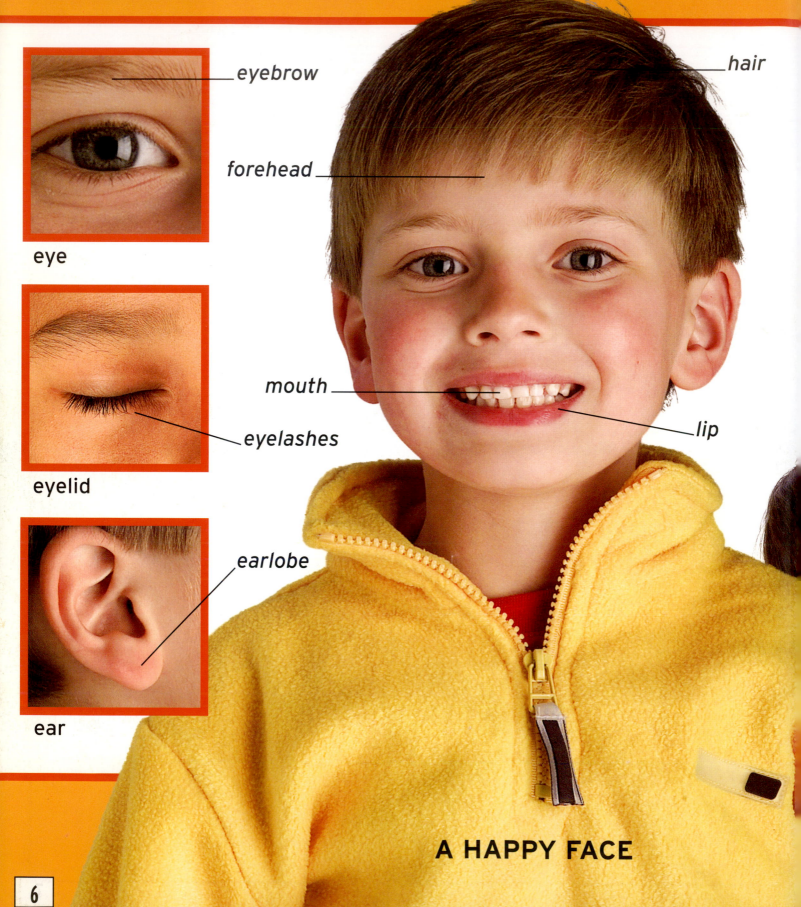

eyebrow

hair

eye

forehead

eyelashes

eyelid

mouth

lip

earlobe

ear

A HAPPY FACE

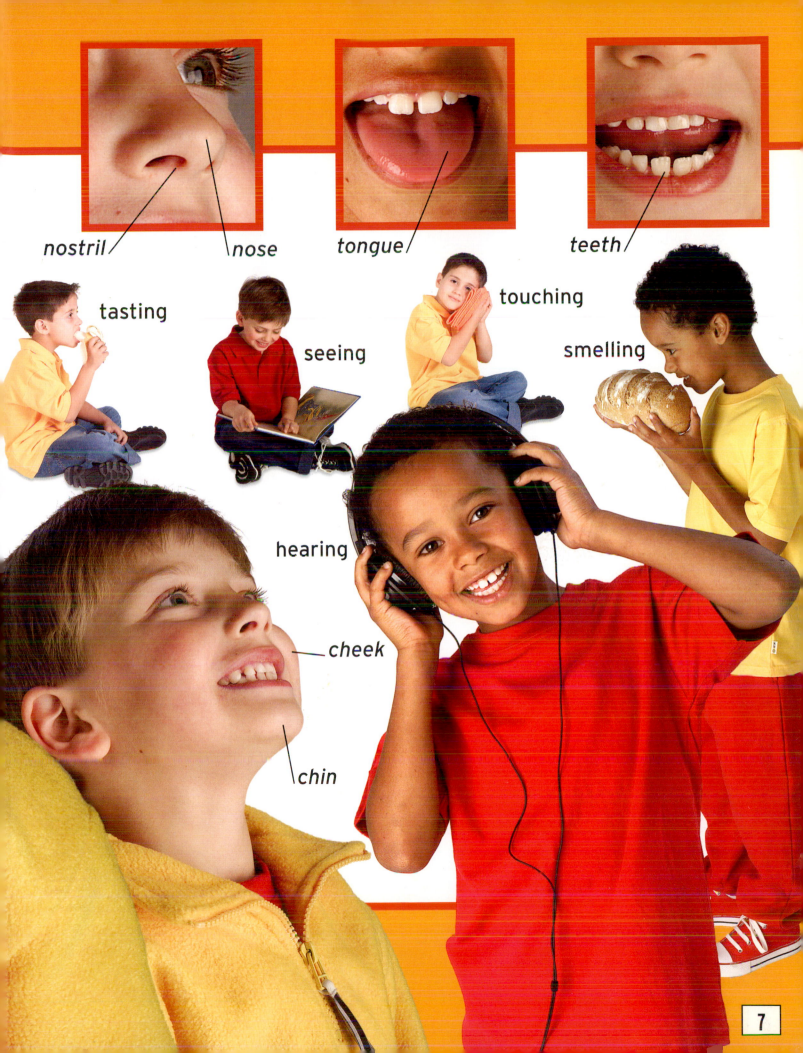

nostril nose tongue teeth

tasting seeing touching smelling

hearing cheek chin

THE
Body

head

shoulder

neck

arm

chest

abdomen

finger

wrist

waist

hand

hip

8

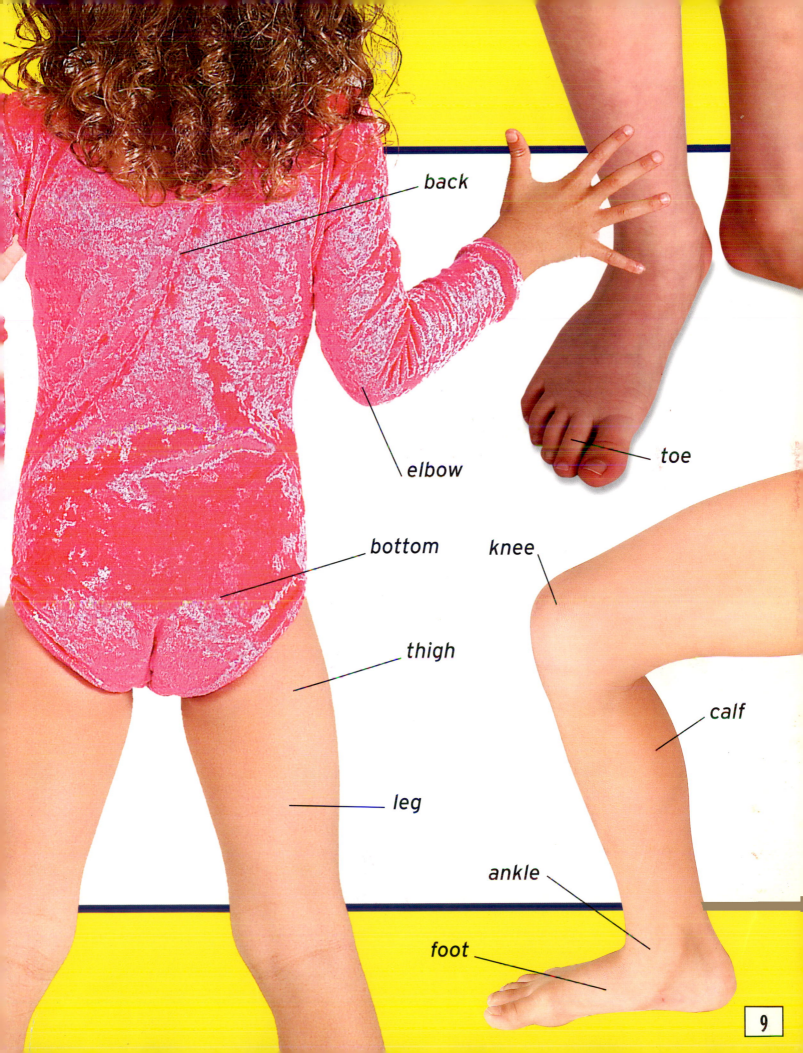

back

elbow

toe

bottom

knee

thigh

calf

leg

ankle

foot

9

MY Family

my birth certificate

my brother

my pa

my kitten

my nana

my twin

ME

10

BABY
CHILD
TEENAGER
ADULT
MY SURNAME
Simpson.

my uncle

my photo album

my aunt

my cousin

my father

my grandmother

my grandfather

my mother

my sister

11

BABY'S Things

bootees

blanket

pins

high chair

rattle

cotton balls

soft toy

powder

monitors

BIB

bottle

pacifier

potty

diaper

jumpsuit

mobile

wipes

stroller

cot

car seat

13

Clothes

tights

shorts

sweater

overalls

jeans

singlet

BOOTS

coat

tie

trousers

underpants

shoes

14

T-shirt

dress

skirt

leotard

shirt

socks

underpants

jacket

sneakers

15

Accessories

satchel

hat

hairclip

key ring

beret

braces

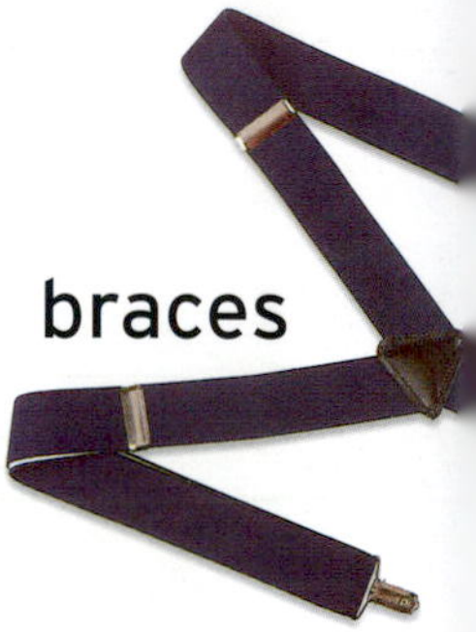

EARRING

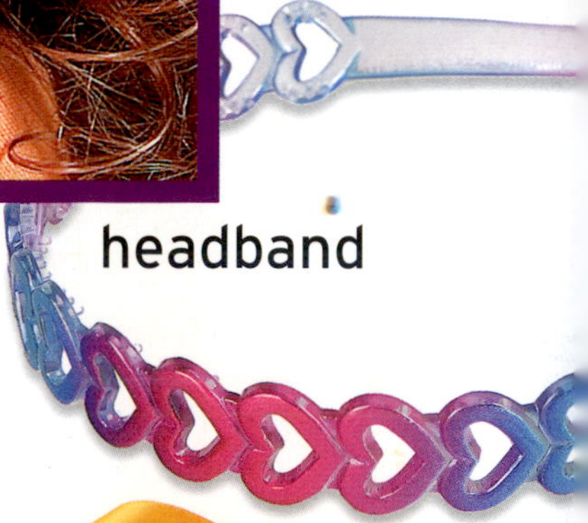

headband

ribbons

16

necklace

scrunchies

backpack

handbag

evening bag

belt

gloves

watch

cap

rings

fake tattoo

bracelets

17

Food

egg

sandwich

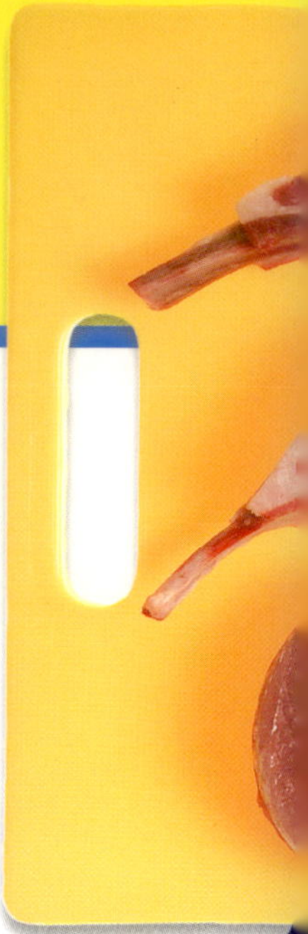

sugar

butter

cereal

juice

yogurt

FISH

granola bars

bread

crackers

hot chocolate

oatmeal

milk

cheese

meat

rice

pasta

honey

salad

19

PARTY
Food

muffin

fried chicken

fruit tart

potato
chips

pies

JELLYBEANS

donut

popcorn

lollipop

jello

cookies

marshmallows

candy cane

nuts

cake

chocolate

soda

pizza

hamburger

fries

Fruit

raspberry

cherries

tomato

kiwi fruit

avocado

grapefruit

ORANGES

pear

banana

apricot

mangoes

olives

22

mandarin
orange

strawberry

dates

pineapple

apple

lemon

watermelon

grapes

peaches

Vegetables

asparagus

onion

cabbages

leeks

carrots

SWEET CORN

cauliflower

radish

spinach

mushrooms

rhubarb

broccoli

zucchini

parsnip

beet

lettuce

green onions

turnip

potatoes

eggplant

peas

25

Plants

acorns

fern

grass

holly

ivy

LEAVES

blossom

cactus

seedling

pine cone

26

moss

trunk

bark

bottlebrush

wattle

gum flowers

palm tree

weeping willow

maple

oak leaves

flytrap

pot plants

27

Flowers

pansy

violet

bouquet

daisy

chrysanthemum

orchid

bluebell

SUNFLOWER

tulip

knotweed

gardenia

cornflower

zinnia

carnation

hibiscus

marigold

iris

rose

lily

gerbera

freesia

Gardening

trowel

potting mix

gardening gloves

shears

faucet

spade

SHED

hose

bulbs

watering can

seeds

compost bin

flowerpots

clippers

gardening hat

wheelbarrow

lawnmower

rake

shovel

weeds

rock

LARGE
Mammals

cheetah

tiger

lion

elephant

bear

WHALE

hippopotamus

seal

rhinoceros

polar bear

deer

monkey

dolphins

kangaroo

camel

leopard

giraffe

chimpanzee

puma

gorilla

moose

SMALL Mammals

hedgehog

rat

squirrel

otter

raccoon

meerkats

BADGER

koala

opossum

34

fox

echidna

skunk

wombat

chipmunk

hare

opossum

wolverine

bat

beaver

Tasmanian devil

armadillo

Birds

emu

pigeon

owl

kingfisher

puffin

parrot

ALBATROSS

eagle

macaw

pelican

ostrich

falcon

hawk

lovebird

flamingo

crane

peacock

toucan

swans

vulture

woodpecker

REPTILES AND
Amphibians

bullfrog

alligator

skink

iguana

gecko

KOMODO DRAGON

cobra

tortoise

terrapin

toad

38

salamanders

corn snake

rattlesnake

python

boa

treefrog

chameleon

turtle

milk snake

monitor lizard

crocodile

WATER Animals

puffer fish

lobster

tuna

herrings

oysters

prawn

stingray

JELLYFISH

angelfish

seadragon

coral

40

shark

damsel fish

cod

sardines

salmon

starfish

sea horse

catfish

crab

eel

pike

Mini-beasts

dragonfly

grasshopper

ladybird

fly

centipede

moth

ANTS

spider

praying mantis

cockroach

leaf insect

bee

42

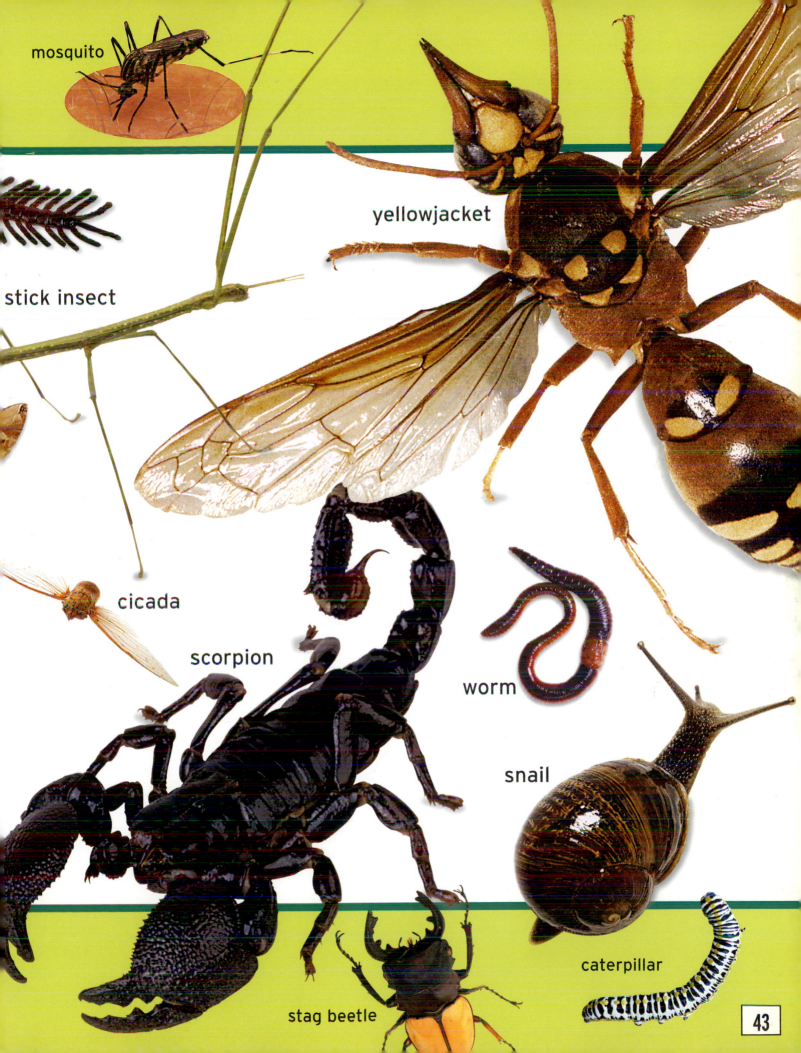

mosquito

stick insect

yellowjacket

cicada

scorpion

worm

snail

stag beetle

caterpillar

ANIMAL Bodies

feathers

hoof

horn

wings

fur

FANGS

tail

spines

talons

whiskers

scales

paw

claws

gill

mane

snout

antlers

pouch

tusks

fin

beak

45

Pets

exercise wheel

mice

lead

hamster

dog

AQUARIUM

ferret

guinea pig

cat

canary

46

pony

kennel

collar

tug toy

rabbit

goldfish

cage

stable

saddle

scratching post

pet bed

A House

door knocker

mailbox

balcony

window

curtain

lawn

doormat

lock

wall

blind

door

porch

gutter

bricks

fence

garage

drive

roof

trash can

doorknob

IN THE
Bedroom

chest of drawers

night-light

photo frame

quilt

pillow

alarm clock

toy box

trophy

BED

books

The Folk of the FARAWAY Tree

dressing gown

wardrobe

50

slippers

hobby horse

pajamas

mattress

hat tree

teddy bear

rug

poster

51

IN THE
Bathroom

toilet

hairbrush

rubber duck

shampoo

facecloth

WASHBASIN

plug

make-up

52

medicine

tissues

comb

toilet paper

toothpaste

hairdryer

shower

mirror

towel

bath

toothbrush

soap

bubble bath

IN THE
Family Room

lamp

video recorder

coffee table

remote control

rocking chair

cushion

BOOKSHELF

vase

television

compact disc

video cassettes

picture

carpet

beanbag

games table

coasters

headphones

sofa

newspaper

stereo

magazines

IN THE
Kitchen

juicer

kitchen scales

electric mixer

oven

cooktop

apron

toaster

BENCHTOP

stool

refrigerator

food processor

56

table

breadboard

chair

jar

breadmaker

kettle

cookbook

sink

dishwasher

microwave oven

57

IN THE
Cupboard

bowl

saucepan

cake tin

plate

detergent

PLATTER

cup

sponge

teapot

dishtowel

rubber gloves

rolling pin

wooden spoon

glass

fork

knife

spoon

tray

egg-beater

fry pan

jug

59

IN THE
Study

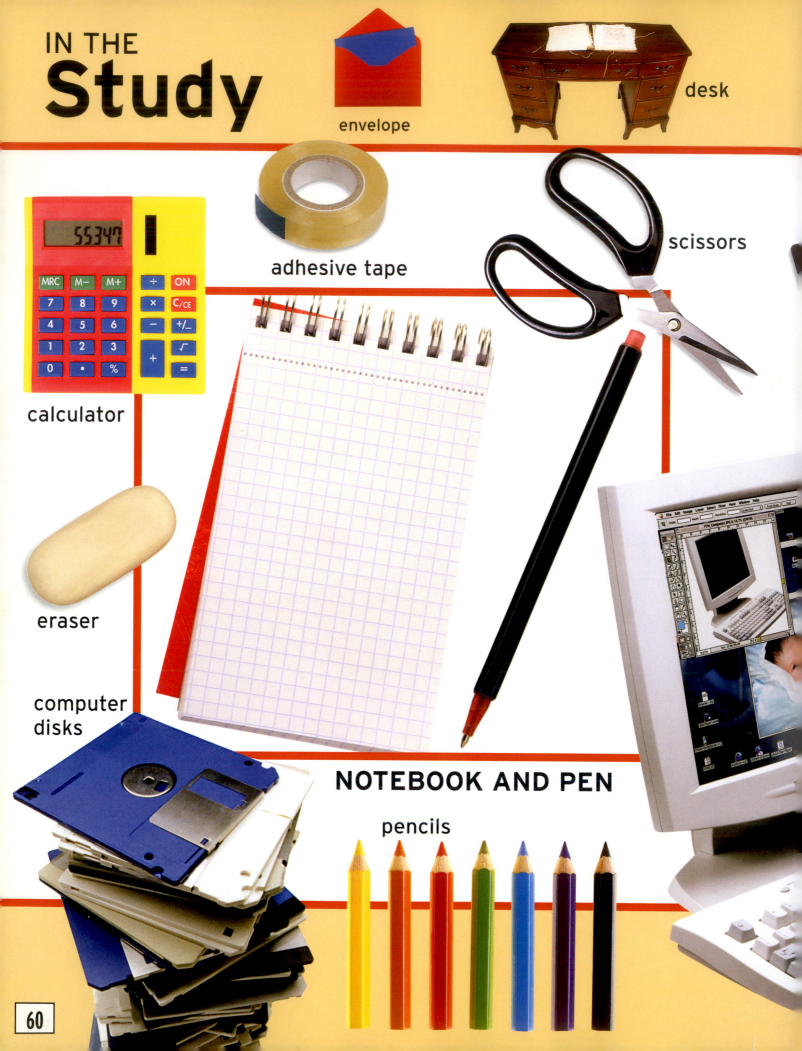

envelope

desk

adhesive tape

scissors

calculator

eraser

computer disks

NOTEBOOK AND PEN

pencils

dictionary

stapler

diary

telephone

desk chair

sharpener

paper clip

computer

ruler

paper

glue

61

HOUSEHOLD Items

nails

pliers

screw

ax

coat-hanger

power point

vacuum cleaner

WASHING MACHINE

saw

hammer

wrench

tape measure

paintbrush

screwdrivers

iron

dryer

ironing board

ladder

tool kit

paint tin

electric drill

63

Birthday Party

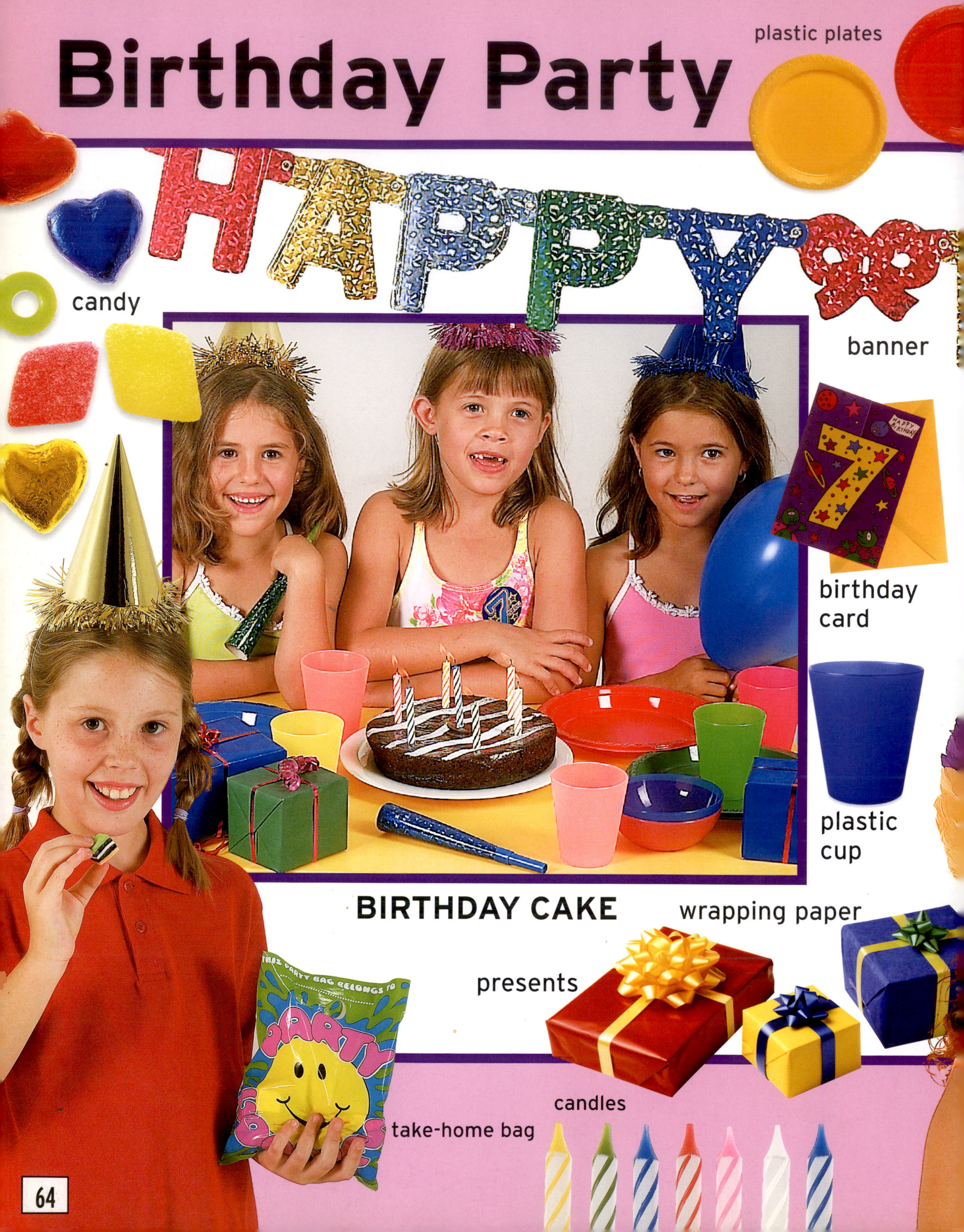
plastic plates
HAPPY
candy
banner
birthday card
plastic cup
BIRTHDAY CAKE
wrapping paper
presents
candles
take-home bag

streamers

fruit drink

bow

party whistles

invitation

BIRTHDAY

straws

badge

paper hat

birthday girl

7 today

friends

mask

party game

65

Fancy Dress

wand

bumblebee

glitter

Little
Bo Peep

king

butterfly

mouse

octopus

flower

puss

tiara

fairy wings

sea lion

costume

bunny

starfish

puppy

calf

pirate

wig

clown

67

Toys

dice

doll's house

wagon

dinosaur

soldier

PUZZLE

dragon

blackboard

cowboy

checkerboard

cube

skipping rope

doll

cards

spaceship

robot

tricycle

blocks

slinky

dominoes

marbles

69

FAVORITE Things

jewelry

kite

boomerang

money

crayons

piggy bank

penguin

SEE-SAW

telescope

ukulele

stickers

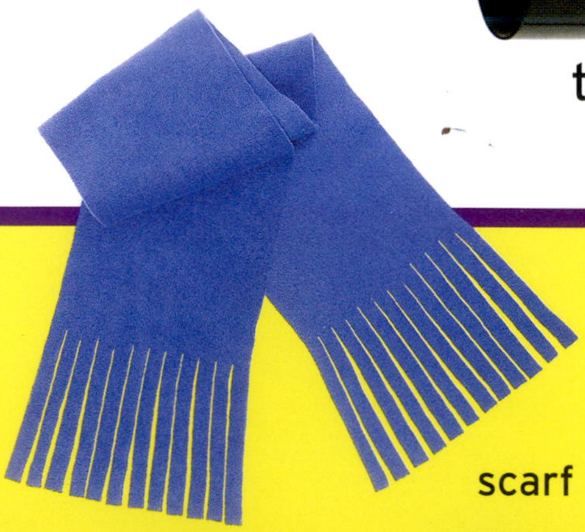

scarf

magnet

quilt

fishing rod

chess set

coconut

Frisbee

tutu

radio

yo-yo

SPORTS Equipment

basketball

rollerblades

baseball glove

bicycle helmet

cricket bat

dartboard

sailboard

flippers

SURFBOARD

soccer ball

baseball bat

ice skates

72

whistle

skis

stopwatch

darts

bicycle

30
28
26
58
15
24
56
12
54
9
6
22
52
50
20
48
1/10
18
46
16

goggles

football

wetsuit

tennis racket

hockey stick

73

MUSICAL Instruments

bells

flute

clarinet

triangle

harp

ACOUSTIC GUITAR

cello

maracas

xylophone

piano

recorder

accordion

banjo

tambourine

trumpet

cymbals

saxophone

bagpipes

drums

electric guitar

violin

ON THE
Farm

scarecrow

horse

foal

hen

chick

pig

donkey

duck

SHEEPDOG

lamb

rooster

76

tractor

cow

farmer

goat

farmhouse

sheep

field

goose

hay bale

gate

77

AT THE
Beach

ice cream

beach ball

deckchair

seaweed

sunscreen

ROCK POOL

swim ring

shells

sea

bucket
and spade

sandcastle

beach
umbrella

sand

seagull

sailboat

swimsuit

sunhat

drink

sandals

basket

sunglasses

79

Camping

hiking boot

camp bed

trail mix

Swiss army knife

binoculars

thermos

MAP

gas lamp

camping stove

compass

rope

matches

batteries

foot pump

air-bed

rucksack

flashlight

tent

sleeping bag

camera

first-aid kit

Transport

helicopter

bus

ambulance

cab

wheelchair

BOAT

motorcycle

truck

fire engine

scooter

jet ski

car

ship

airplane

skateboard

yacht

hot-air balloon

racing car

submarine

train

PEOPLE at Work

electrician

chef

sailor

ballerina

doctor

scientist

FIREFIGHTERS

artist

decorator

detective

84

judge

soccer player

plumber

boxer

waiter

astronaut

builder

nurse

office worker

teacher

Actions

walking

climbing

drawing

talking

hugging

sitting

HIDING

crying

reading

drinking

sleeping

running

playing

cutting

eating

kicking

jumping

frowning

reaching

writing

laughing

Opposites

open

closed

fat

dry

thin

wet

under

over

push

pull

down

up

young

old

short

long

empty

full

big

clean

small

dirty

89

Numbers

1 one **2** two **3** three **4** four **5** five

9 nine **10** ten **11** eleven

15 fifteen **16** sixteen **17** seventeen

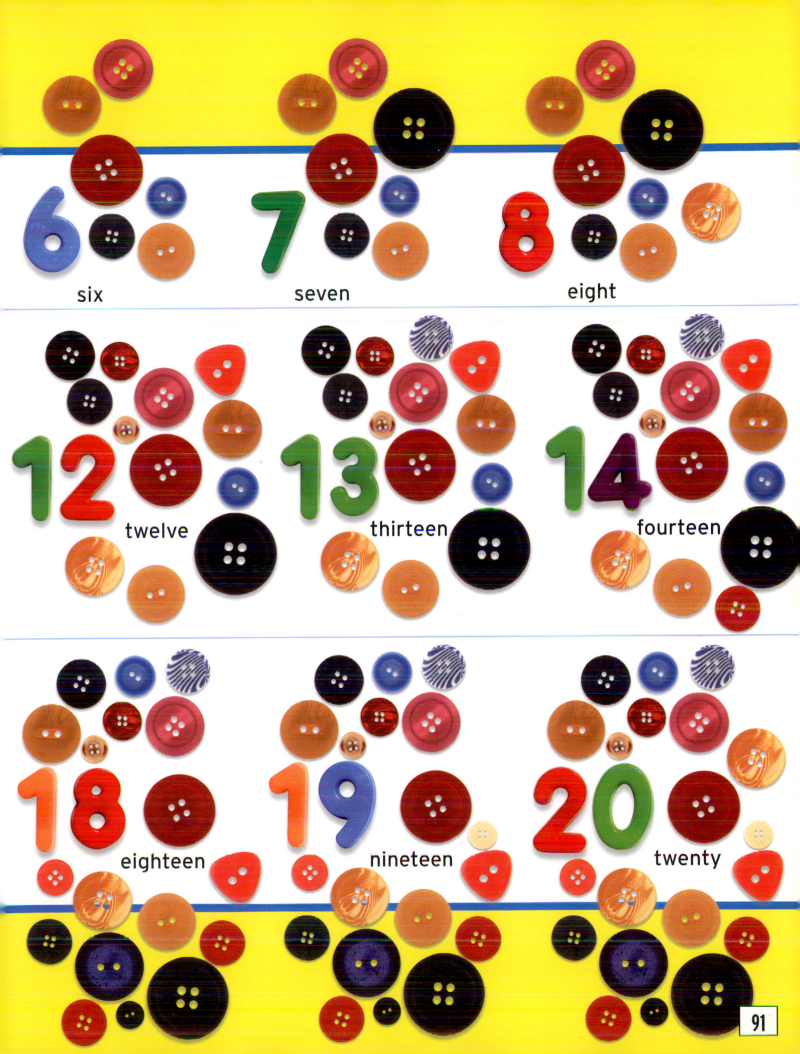

6 six

7 seven

8 eight

12 twelve

13 thirteen

14 fourteen

18 eighteen

19 nineteen

20 twenty

COLORS
and Shapes

red

black

orange

crescent

yellow

SQUARE

triangle

gray

heart

92

oval

pink

diamond

blue

purple

green

rectangle

circle

brown

star

white

93

Flags

The Netherlands

Canada

Belgium

Mexcio

Phillipines

Australia

Singapore

Hungary

The Czech
Republic

Norway

Poland

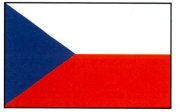

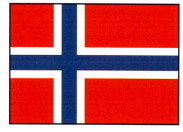

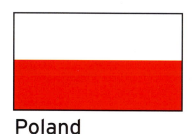

South Korea

Finland

United Kingdom

Egypt

Brazil

South Africa

Germany

Ukraine

Switzerland

Greece

Russian
Federation

Saudi Arabia

India

Italy

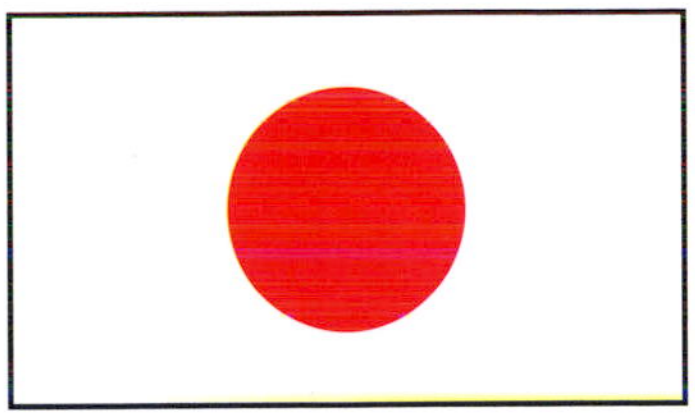

Japan

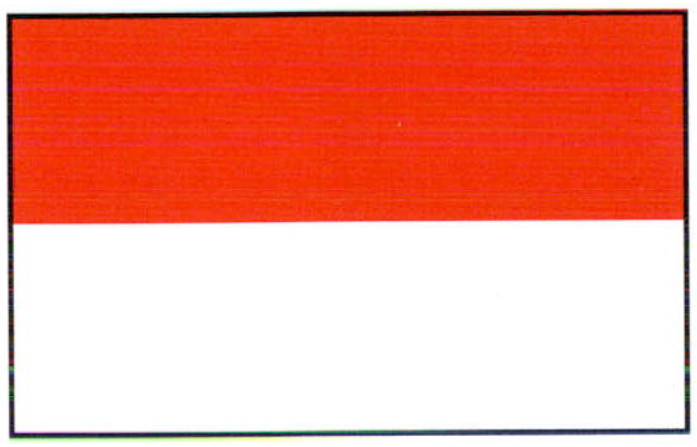

Indonesia

Sweden

Spain

Denmark

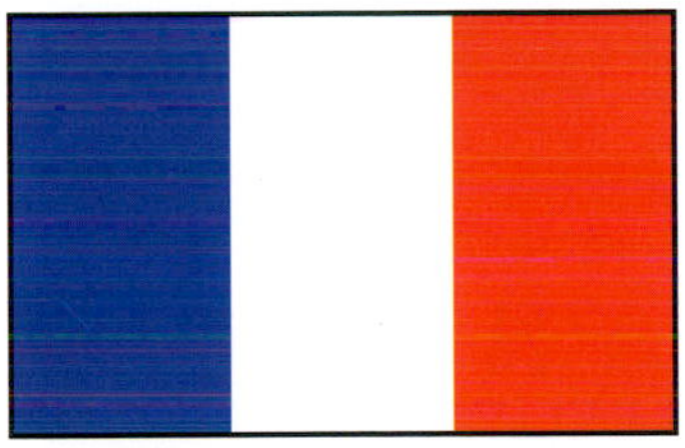

France

Chile

New Zealand

China

United Sates of
America

THE Earth and Sky

clouds

Earth

forest

MOUNTAIN

wind

lightning

96

desert

eclipse

rain

iceberg

river

moon

pond

rainbow

stars

storm

sun

volcano

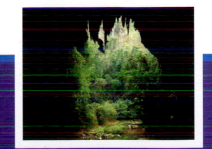

cave

waterfall

pasture

FIRST PICTURE
DICTIONARY

Archie Oliver

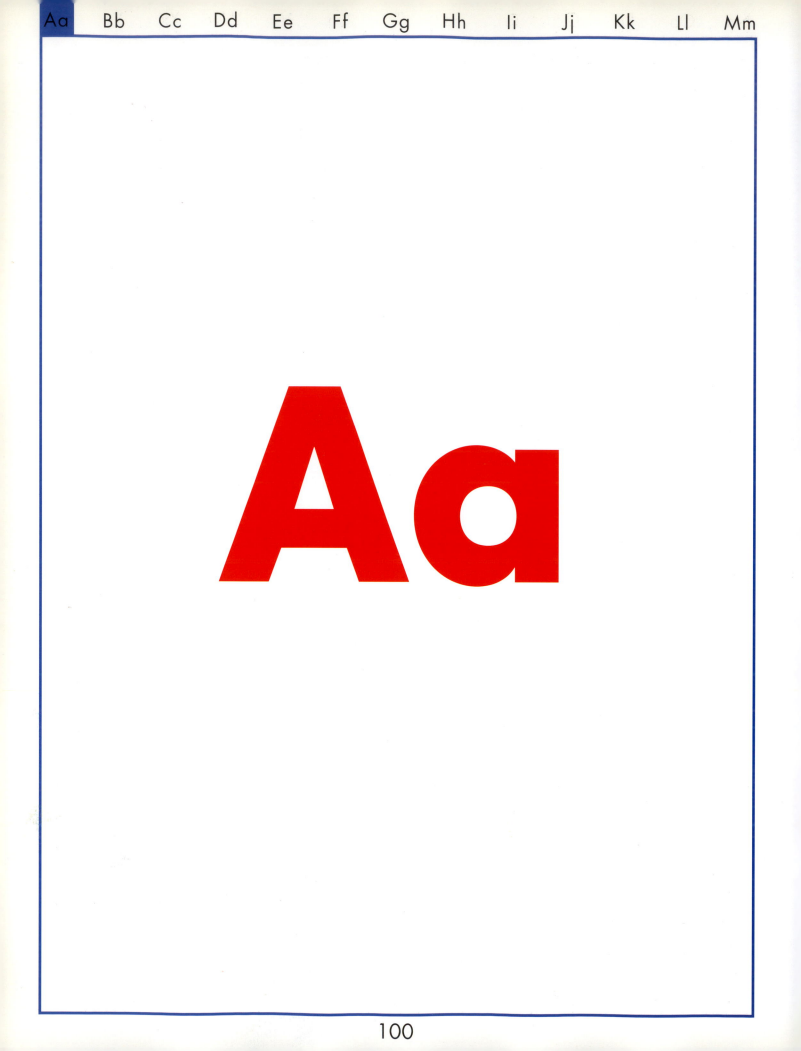

Aa

able

To be **able** to do something means you can do it. Luke is **able** to swim two laps of the pool.

above

Above means over or in a higher place. Birds fly in the sky **above** us.

accident

An **accident** is something that happens by mistake. Falling off your bicycle is an **accident**.

acorn

An **acorn** is a nut that grows on an oak tree.

acrobat

An **acrobat** is a person who does tricks like flips and somersaults. Many **acrobats** can swing on a trapeze and walk on a tightrope.

across

Across means from one side to another. There is a bridge **across** the river.

actor

An **actor** is a person whose job it is to pretend to be someone else. You see **actors** on television, in films, and in plays.

add

1. To **add** means to put two or more things together. Philippa **adds** milk to her breakfast cereal. 2. To **add** means to find the sum of two or more numbers.

$$3+3=6$$

address

Jenny Star
22 Movie Street
Hollywood, CA 90028

An **address** is the place where a person lives. An **address** includes the number or name of a building, the name of the street, the town or city, and a special number code.

adult

An **adult** is a grown-up man or woman. Children grow up to become **adults**.

afraid

To be **afraid** is to fear someone or something. Alexandra is **afraid** of spiders.

again

Again means once more. Lachlan read his favorite comic on Saturday. He read it **again** on Sunday.

age

Your **age** is how old you are. Charlotte is six years of **age**.

ahead

To be **ahead** is to be in front of someone or something. Lauren is running **ahead** of Dean.

air

Air is a gas that is all around us. People breathe **air**. You cannot see **air**.

airplane

An **airplane** is a flying machine with wings and engines. An **airplane** carries people or objects from place to place.

airport

An **airport** is a place where people catch airplanes. Airplanes take off and land at **airports**.

alarm

An **alarm** is a loud sound. It warns of danger, or tells a person it is time to do something. Shelley set the **alarm** on her clock to ring at seven o'clock in the morning.

album

An **album** is a blank book that people put photographs or stamps in.

alike

To be **alike** means to look like each other. These children are dressed **alike**.

alive

Alive means living and not dead.

all

All means every or the whole of. Luke ate **all** his dinner.

alligator

An **alligator** is a large animal with scaly skin, strong jaws and sharp teeth. It has four legs and a powerful tail.

almond

An **almond** is a nut. Almonds grow on trees.

alone

To be **alone** is to be on your own. After his friends left, Dean was **alone** in the room.

alphabet

An **alphabet** is a list of the letters used to spell words. There are twenty-six letters in the **alphabet**.

abcdefghi
jklmnopqr
stuvwxyz

ambulance

An **ambulance** is a vehicle that takes sick or injured people to hospital.

anchor

An **anchor** is a heavy iron hook that is chained to a ship. It is dropped to the bottom of the sea to stop the ship from floating away.

angry

To be **angry** is to feel mad or cross.

animal

An **animal** is any living thing that can move itself. **Animals** can run, hop, fly, crawl, swim, and walk. Insects, fish, frogs, snakes, birds, cows, dogs, and human beings are all **animals**.

ankle

Your **ankle** is the part of your body that joins your foot to your leg.

another

Another means one more. Lauren had **another** bite of the banana.

ant

An **ant** is an insect. **Ants** live in large groups called colonies.

antler

An **antler** is a type of hard horn on the head of a deer. **Antlers** grow in pairs. **Antlers** can look like the branches of a tree.

ape

An **ape** is an animal that looks like a large monkey without a tail. An **ape** has long arms and can stand on two feet.

appear

To **appear** means to come into view. Luke suddenly **appeared** in the doorway.

apple

An **apple** is a round fruit. **Apples** grow on trees and can be red, green, or yellow.

apricot

An **apricot** is a soft yellow fruit. It looks like a small peach. **Apricots** grow on trees.

apron

An **apron** is a piece of clothing that a person wears to protect the clothes underneath. Isaac wears an **apron** when he cooks.

aquarium

An **aquarium** is a glass tank filled with water. Pet fish live in **aquariums**.

arm

Your **arm** is the part of your body between your hand and shoulder. You have two **arms**.

armor

Armor is a hard covering that protects the body. Long ago, knights wore suits of **armor** during battle.

arrow

An **arrow** is a sign that points in one direction. The **arrow** pointed to the exit.

artist

An **artist** is a person who makes beautiful things. Some **artists** draw or paint pictures. Sculptors and woodcarvers are also **artists**.

ask

To **ask** means to speak a question. The teacher **asked** Talullah to spell her name.

asleep

If you are **asleep**, you are sleeping.

astronaut

An **astronaut** is a person who travels or works in space. **Astronauts** have walked on the moon.

athlete

An **athlete** is a person who plays sport. Some **athletes** play sport in teams.

atlas

An **atlas** is a book of maps.

attack

To **attack** means to hurt someone or damage something on purpose.

author

An **author** is a person who writes stories, poems, and plays.

autograph

An **autograph** is a person's signature. Ashleigh collects **autographs** of famous people.

avocado

An **avocado** is a green fruit. It is shaped like a pear.

awake

You are **awake** when you are not asleep.

award

An **award** is a special prize.

AWARD

CERTIFICATE FOR EXCELLENCE

Congratulations

Pat Mantley

our most recent Recipient of Excellence
in
Master with Specialized Study

ax

An **ax** is a tool with a long handle and a sharp head. Patrick chopped wood with an **ax**.

Bb

baby
A **baby** is a very young child or animal.

back
Your **back** is the part of your body that is behind you. Your **back** goes from your neck to your bottom.

bad
Bad means naughty or not good. It is **bad** manners to poke your tongue out at people.

badge
A **badge** is a small piece of tin, plastic, or material that is pinned or sewn onto clothing.

bag
A **bag** is a container made of paper, plastic, or leather. **Bags** are used to carry or hold things.

ball
A **ball** is a round object made of rubber, plastic, or leather. People play games with **balls**. You can kick, bounce, roll, and throw **balls**.

ballerina
A **ballerina** is a girl or woman who dances in a ballet.

balloon
A **balloon** is a small rubber bag that floats when it is filled with air or gas. Darcy blew up **balloons** for his birthday party.

banana

A **banana** is a long, curved fruit. It has a yellow skin and a soft center. **Bananas** grow in bunches on trees.

band

A **band** is a group of singers and musicians who perform together. Do you have a favorite pop **band**?

bandage

A **bandage** is a piece of material that is wrapped around a wound. A **bandage** keeps a wound clean and helps it to heal.

bank

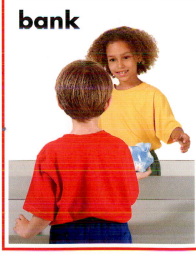

A **bank** is a place where people keep their money. People can also take their money out of a **bank**. A **bank** keeps a person's money safe.

baseball

Baseball is a popular sport. **Baseball** is played by two teams with a bat and a ball.

basket

A **basket** is a wooden container for holding or carrying things. Elizabeth put her shopping in a **basket**.

bat

1. A **bat** is a wooden club used to hit a ball. A **bat** is used in baseball and other sports. 2. A **bat** is a small animal with wings. **Bats** sleep during the day and fly at night.

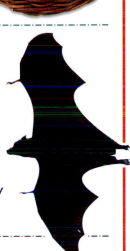

bath

A **bath** is a tub filled with water. People sit in a **bath** and wash themselves.

battery

A **battery** is an object that makes power for a piece of electrical equipment. Laura put a **battery** in her torch. Zane's portable radio runs on **batteries**.

beach

A **beach** is a sandy area beside the sea. Lachlan is building a sandcastle on the **beach**.

bead

A **bead** is a small ball of stone, wood or plastic with a hole through the middle. Michelle put **beads** on a string to make a bracelet.

beak

A **beak** is the hard, horny part of a bird's mouth. A toucan has a large **beak**.

bean

A **bean** is a small green vegetable.

bear

A **bear** is a large animal with sharp claws, a thick coat, and powerful jaws. A **bear** eats fish, plants, and fruit.

beard

A **beard** is hair that grows on a man's chin and cheeks.

beautiful

Beautiful means attractive to look at. The field is full of **beautiful** flowers.

beaver

A **beaver** is a small animal that lives in a dam in a river.

bed

A **bed** is a piece of furniture that a person sleeps or rest on. **Beds** are usually in bedrooms.

bee

A **bee** is a small flying insect. Some **bees** make honey from the liquid inside flowers. Some **bees** can sting.

beetle

A **beetle** is an insect with four wings.

begin

To **begin** is to start something. When the music **begins**, the children start to sing.

behind

Behind means at the back of. Charlotte is standing **behind** the wooden block.

bell

A **bell** is a metal cup with a clapper inside it. When the **bell** is shaken, the clapper hits the inside of the cup, and the **bell** rings.

belong

To **belong** means to be someone's possession. The orange ball **belongs** to Lauren.

below

Below means beneath. Luke is above. Lauren is **below**.

belt

A **belt** is a leather or plastic strap worn around the waist. Joseph wears a **belt** to hold up his trousers.

bend

To **bend** means to stoop or to make a curve. Talullah is **bending** over to pick up her teddy bear.

beneath

Beneath means under or below. Jordan is sitting **beneath** an umbrella.

berry

A **berry** is a fruit. Raspberries, strawberries, and blackberries are all **berries**.

between

Between means in the middle of. Alexandra is sitting **between** a yellow and a green chair.

beware

Beware means to be on the alert for danger. **Beware** of the guard dog!

bicycle

A **bicycle** is a vehicle with two wheels, two pedals, brakes, and handlebars. People ride **bicycles**.

binoculars

Binoculars are special eyeglasses that make things that are far away look close.

bird

A **bird** is an animal with feathers, wings, and a beak. Most **birds** can fly.

birthday

January						
Sunday	Monday	Tuesday	Wednesday	Thursday	Friday	Saturday
1	2	3	4	5	6	7
8	9	10	11	12	13	14
15	16	17	18	19	20	21
22	23	24	25	26	27	28
29	30	31				

Your **birthday** is the day you were born. Leslie was born on January 19, 1995. Her **birthday** is January 19.

bite

To **bite** is to grip and cut food with your teeth.

black

Black is the darkest of all colors. A car tire is **black**.

blanket

A **blanket** is a large cloth. Sally puts an extra **blanket** on her bed in winter to keep herself warm.

blind

Blind means unable to see. Some **blind** people use a white stick to help them find their way. Others have special dogs that guide them.

block

A **block** is a piece of wood, stone, or plastic with straight sides. William played with his toy **blocks**.

blood

Blood is the red liquid inside your body. Your heart pumps **blood** around your body.

blossom

A **blossom** is a flower that grows on a tree or bush.

blow

To **blow** means to push air out of your mouth. Can you **blow** up a balloon?

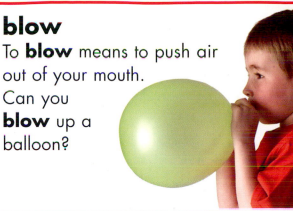

blue

Blue is a color. The sky is **blue**.

boat

A **boat** is a vessel. A **boat** carries people and objects across water.

body

Your **body** is every bit of you. Your **body** is made of bones, skin, hair, muscles, blood, and other things. Your head, neck, chest, arms, legs, and bottom are all parts of your **body**.

boil

To **boil** is to heat a liquid until it bubbles and steams. People often **boil** water in a kettle.

bone

A **bone** is a part of your skeleton. There are more than 200 **bones** in your body. **Bones** link together to make up your skeleton.

book

A **book** is an object that has printed pages and a cover. People read **books** to learn about things. People also read **books** for fun.

boot

A **boot** is a kind of shoe with high sides. Tommy walked through the puddles in his **boots**. His feet stayed dry.

bottle

A **bottle** is a glass or plastic container that holds liquids.

bottom

1. **Bottom** means the lowest place or part.
2. Your **bottom** is a part of your body. Lauren is sitting on her **bottom**.

bow

1. To **bow** is to bend downwards from the waist. At the end of the play, the actors took a **bow**. 2. A **bow** is a weapon used to shoot arrows.

bowl

A **bowl** is an open container made of glass or plastic. A **bowl** is used to hold food or liquids.

box

A **box** is a wooden, plastic, or cardboard container with straight sides and a flat bottom. A **box** can have a lid. Omar keeps his toys in a large **box**.

boy

A **boy** is a male child. A **boy** grows into a man.

bracelet

A **bracelet** is a piece of jewelry. It is a band or chain worn around the wrist. Sharon is wearing a pretty **bracelet** made of beads.

brain

Your **brain** is a part of your body. It is inside your skull. You think, learn and feel with your **brain**. Your **brain** makes the different parts of your body work.

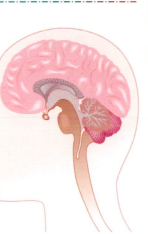

bread

Bread is a food made from flour, water and other things. **Bread** is baked in an oven.

break

To **break** means to smash into pieces. A plate will usually **break** when it is dropped on the floor.

breakfast

Breakfast is a meal eaten in the morning. At **breakfast**, some people eat cereal.

brick

A **brick** is a hard building block. Thousands of **bricks** are used to build a house. **Bricks** are made of clay.

bridge

A **bridge** is something that is built over a river, railway, or road, so that people can cross.

brooch

A **brooch** is a piece of jewelry that is pinned onto clothing.

brother

A **brother** is a boy or man who has the same parents as another person. Harry and Luke are **brothers**. They have the same father and mother.

brown

Brown is a dark color. Chocolate is **brown**.

brush

A **brush** is a wooden or plastic object with bristles. Libby uses a **brush** to keep her hair tidy.

bubble

A **bubble** is a hollow ball made of liquid or chewing gum. Talullah is blowing **bubbles**.

bucket

A **bucket** is a plastic or metal container with a handle. **Buckets** are used to carry things.

bud

A **bud** is a tiny shoot that grows on a plant or tree. A **bud** turns into a flower, a leaf, or a branch.

build

To **build** means to make something by joining things together. Lachlan likes to **build** towers with his blocks.

building

A **building** is a place that has a roof, walls, and a door. A house is a **building**.

bulldozer

A **bulldozer** is a large, powerful tractor with a blade at the front. A **bulldozer** is used to move earth and rocks.

burn

To **burn** means to be on fire. When a match is lit, it **burns**.

bus

A **bus** is a large vehicle with an engine, wheels, doors, windows, and many seats. A **bus** travels from place to place, picking up and dropping off passengers.

116

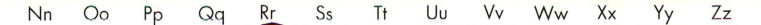

butcher

A **butcher** is a person who cuts up meat to sell.

butter

Butter is a food made from cream. It is soft and yellow. Some people like to spread **butter** on bread.

butterfly

A **butterfly** is an insect with large, colorful wings. A **butterfly** starts life as a caterpillar.

button

A **button** is a little round object that is sewn onto clothing. **Buttons** are used to close a shirt or a jacket.

buy

To **buy** means to pay money for something. Luke is using his allowance to **buy** some fruit.

Cc

cactus

A **cactus** is a plant with a thick skin and sharp spines. A **cactus** grows in a desert.

cage

A **cage** is a box with sides made of bars. Paul keeps his pet birds in a **cage**.

cake

A **cake** is a sweet food made with flour, sugar, eggs, and milk. It is baked in an oven.

calendar

A **calendar** is a chart that shows the days and months of the year.

camel

A **camel** is a large animal. It has a long neck, four legs, and one or two humps on its back. Some **camels** work in the desert. They carry people and goods on their backs.

camera

A **camera** is a machine that takes photographs. Tracey takes a photograph of Archie with her **camera**.

can

1. **Can** means to be able to do something. Phillip **can** swim. Moira **can** dance. 2. A **can** is a metal container. Arthur opens a **can** of tomatoes.

candle

A **candle** is a stick of wax. It has a string, called a wick, inside it. A **candle** gives off light when the wick is lit.

canoe

A **canoe** is a small, narrow boat. A person moves a **canoe** through the water with a paddle.

car

A **car** is a vehicle that carries people over roads. A **car** has an engine, four wheels, windows, and seats for a driver and passengers.

card

A **card** is a folded piece of paper with words or pictures on it. Penelope sent a birthday **card** to her friend.

carrot

A **carrot** is an orange vegetable. It grows under the ground.

carry

To **carry** means to lift and move something from one place to another. Dean **carries** his books to class.

118

castle

A **castle** is a large building with high walls, towers, and big gates. Long ago, kings and queens lived in **castles**.

cat

A **cat** is an animal with four legs, a tail, claws, whiskers, and fur. **Cats** are popular pets. Lions, tigers, and leopards are called big **cats**.

catch

To **catch** means to take hold of something when it is moving. Alexandra likes to throw and **catch** a ball.

caterpillar

A **caterpillar** is a small animal. It looks like a furry worm with tiny legs. A **caterpillar** turns into a butterfly or moth.

cave

A **cave** is a large hole in a hill, mountain or cliff. Some **caves** are very deep under the ground.

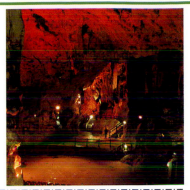

cereal

Cereal is a food. It is made from plants like wheat, rye, and corn. Richard eats a bowl of **cereal** every morning.

chain

A **chain** is a line of metal rings linked together. Imogene is wearing a silver **chain** around her neck. A big **chain** ties a ship to a dock.

chair

A **chair** is a piece of furniture for sitting on. A **chair** has four legs, a back, and a seat.

chalk

Chalk is a soft rock that is used for writing. The teacher writes on the blackboard with a stick of **chalk**.

chase

To **chase** is to run after someone or something to try to catch them. The puppy is **chasing** Talullah.

cheek

Your **cheek** is the part of your face on one side of your nose. You have two **cheeks**.

cheese

Cheese is a food made from milk. **Cheese** is often yellow. Gemma ate a **cheese** sandwich.

cheetah

A **cheetah** is a large wild cat. It has four legs, sharp claws, and a spotted coat. The **cheetah** is the fastest animal on land.

cherry

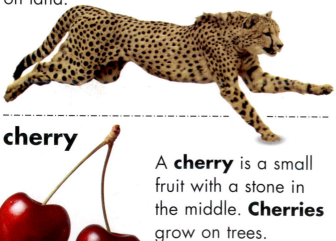

A **cherry** is a small fruit with a stone in the middle. **Cherries** grow on trees.

chest

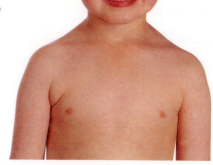

Your **chest** is the front part of your body between your neck and waist. Your **chest** goes in and out when you breathe.

chicken

A **chicken** is a bird. Farmers keep **chickens** for their meat and eggs.

child

A **child** is a young boy or girl.

chimney

A **chimney** is the large tube above a fireplace that lets the smoke out.

chimpanzee

A **chimpanzee** is a wild animal. It looks like a monkey. A **chimpanzee** belongs to the same family as the gorilla.

chin

Your **chin** is the part of your face beneath your mouth. Some **chins** are pointy, some are round.

chocolate

Chocolate is a sweet food. **Chocolate** is made from seeds that grow on cacao trees.

circle

A **circle** is a round shape.

circus

A **circus** is a traveling show. Clowns and acrobats perform in a **circus**. A **circus** takes place in a tent called a Big Top.

city

A **city** is a place where lots of people live and work. A **city** is bigger than a town. New York is a very big **city** in America.

clap

To **clap** means to smack your hands together to make a noise. People **clap** to show they like someone or something. The audience **clapped** at the end of the play.

claw

1. A **claw** is a sharp, curved nail at the end of an animal's foot. 2. A **claw** is one of the sharp pincers on a crab.

clean

To **clean** means to get rid of dirt. Charlotte is **cleaning** her boots.

climb

To **climb** means to move up or down. Dean **climbed** up the ladder, then he **climbed** down.

clock

A **clock** is a machine that shows the time. Some **clocks** have numbers and hands. Some **clocks** just have numbers.

closed

Closed means not open. Charlotte cannot get into the garden because the gate is **closed**.

clothes

Clothes are the things people wear on their bodies. Socks, trousers, dresses, and shirts are all **clothes**.

cloud

A **cloud** is a white or gray pattern in the sky. A **cloud** is made of drops of water. Rain falls from **clouds**.

clown

A **clown** is a person who makes people laugh. **Clowns** often wear costumes.

coat

A **coat** is a piece of warm clothing that goes over other clothes. Rebecca wore a woolen **coat** over her dress.

cobweb

A **cobweb** is a net made of sticky threads. A spider spins a **cobweb** to catch insects to eat.

coconut

A **coconut** is a fruit with a hard shell. There is **coconut** milk inside the shell.

coin

A **coin** is a metal piece of money. Most **coins** are round.

cold

1. **Cold** means without warmth. **Cold** is the opposite of hot. Snow is **cold**. 2. If you have a **cold** you are ill. Lachlan is sneezing because he has a **cold**.

color

Color is a description of what something looks like. Red, blue, green, and white are all **colors**.

comb

A **comb** is a piece of metal or plastic with teeth. A **comb** is used to tidy hair.

compact disc

A **compact disc** is a round object used to store music and information. A **compact disc** is also called a CD.

compass

A **compass** is an instrument that shows the direction in which a person is traveling. Kieran looked at his **compass** to check that he was traveling north.

computer

A **computer** is a machine that stores and shows information. A **computer** can also work out sums. Lauren is writing a story on her **computer**.

continent

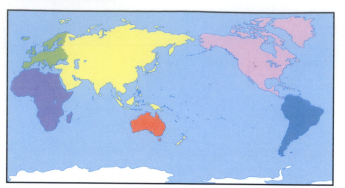

A **continent** is a huge area of land. There are seven **continents**—Asia, Europe, Africa, North America, South America, Australia, and Antarctica.

cook

1. To **cook** means to prepare food for eating by heating it. 2. A **cook** is a person who prepares food for eating.

corn

Corn is a vegetable. **Corn** is usually yellow.

corner

A **corner** is a place where two lines or streets meet. A square has four **corners**.

country

A **country** is a large area of land with its own government. Terry was born in a **country** called Germany.

cow

A **cow** is a female farm animal. **Cows** make milk.

crab

A **crab** is a sea animal with a hard outer shell. **Crabs** have flat bodies with ten legs. They have sharp **claws** on their front legs.

crayon

A **crayon** is a stick of colored wax or chalk that is used for drawing.

crocodile

A **crocodile** is a large Australian animal with scaly skin, strong jaws, and sharp teeth. It has four legs and a powerful tail. A **crocodile** looks like an alligator.

crowd

A **crowd** is a large number of people gathered in one place.

cry

To **cry** means to weep tears. Jordan is **crying** because he is watching a sad movie.

crystal

A **crystal** is a rock-like object that looks like ice.

cub

A **cub** is a baby tiger, lion, bear, wolf, or fox.

cup

A **cup** is a container with a handle on the side. People drink liquids from a **cup**.

cupboard

A **cupboard** is a piece of furniture used for storing things. Mandy put the cups in the **cupboard**.

cut

To **cut** means to open or slice something with a knife or sharp object. Luke **cut** the paper with scissors.

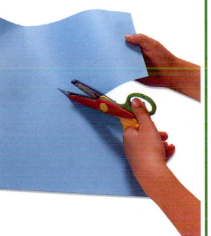

cutlery

Cutlery means the knives, forks, and spoons that people use to eat their food.

Dd

dance

To **dance** means to move your body to music. Luke likes to **dance** with Lauren at the disco.

danger

Danger means at risk of being hurt. You are in **danger** of falling off the cliff if you walk too close to the edge.

DANGER

day

A **day** is a period of time. There are twenty-four hours in one **day**. There are seven **days** in one week—Sunday, Monday, Tuesday, Wednesday, Thursday, Friday, and Saturday.

Thursday 20   Friday 21

deaf

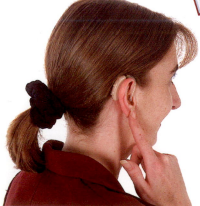

Deaf means not able to hear. Clara wears a hearing aid because she is almost **deaf**.

decide

To **decide** means to choose or make up your mind. Talullah cannot **decide** whether to wear the blue or the red T-shirt.

deer

A **deer** is an animal with four legs. **Deer** live in forests.

dentist

A **dentist** is a person who looks after people's teeth.

desert

A **desert** is an area of very dry land. Very few plants grow in a **desert** because there is so little water.

desk

A **desk** is a piece of furniture that looks like a table.

diamond

1. A **diamond** is a jewel that sparkles in the light. **Diamonds** are very hard and very precious. Tania wears a **diamond** ring on her finger. 2. A **diamond** is a shape with four straight sides.

dice

Dice are small cubes marked with one to six dots. **Dice** are used in games.

dig

Dig means to make a hole in the ground. Alexandra is **digging** with a spade.

dinner

Dinner is the main meal of the day.

dinosaur

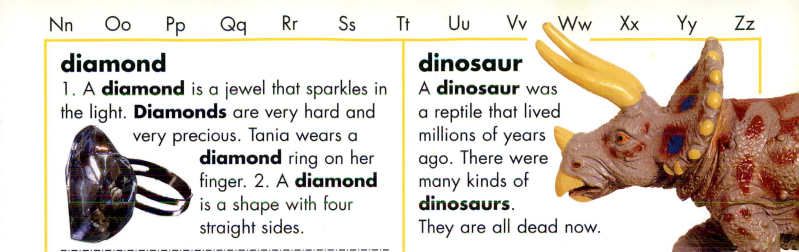

A **dinosaur** was a reptile that lived millions of years ago. There were many kinds of **dinosaurs**. They are all dead now.

dirty

Dirty means not clean. Lachlan has a **dirty** face and hand.

doctor

A **doctor** is a person who looks after people when they are sick or injured.

dog

A **dog** is an animal with four legs and a tail. Many people keep a **dog** as a pet.

doll

A **doll** is a toy that looks like a person. Anna likes to cuddle her **doll**.

dolphin

A **dolphin** is a sea animal that looks like a large fish. **Dolphins** are intelligent and friendly. They live in groups.

donkey

A **donkey** is an animal. It looks like a small horse with big ears. A **donkey** can carry people or goods on its back.

door

A **door** is a large piece of hard material that opens and shuts to form the entrance to a building, room, or cupboard.

dozen

A **dozen** means a set of twelve. Casey picked a **dozen** flowers.

dragonfly

A **dragonfly** is a flying insect with a long body.

draw

To **draw** means to make a picture with a pencil or crayon.

drawer

A **drawer** is a box that slides in and out of a piece of furniture.

dress

A **dress** is a piece of clothing worn by girls and women.

drill

A **drill** is a sharp metal tool that is used to make holes.

drink

To **drink** means to put a liquid into your mouth and swallow it. Luke likes to **drink** a glass of milk after school.

drop

To **drop** means to let something fall, usually by accident. Jordan **dropped** his ice cream.

drum

A **drum** is a musical instrument. It has a hollow body with a tight skin on the top. A person plays a **drum** by beating it with sticks or their hands.

dry

Dry means not wet. Luke's raincoat and umbrella keep him **dry** when it rains.

duck

A **duck** is a water bird. It has short legs and webbed feet. **Ducks** swim on ponds, lakes, and rivers.

Ee

eagle

An **eagle** is a powerful hunting bird. An **eagle** has huge wings, large claws, and a sharp beak.

ear

Your **ear** is the part of your body that you hear with. You have an **ear** on either side of your head.

earth

1. **Earth** is dirt or soil. 2. **Earth** is the name of our planet.

eat

To **eat** means to put food in your mouth, chew it, and swallow it.

egg

An **egg** is a small round or oval object laid by a female animal, such as a bird.

elbow

Your **elbow** is the part of your body that lets your arm bend.

electricity

Electricity is a form of energy. **Electricity** makes things like televisions and lights work. **Electricity** is made at a power station.

elephant

An **elephant** is a very large, strong animal. It has big floppy ears and a trunk. An **elephant** uses its trunk to pick up things.

empty

Empty means has nothing inside. The cup is **empty**.

emu

An **emu** is an Australian bird that looks like an ostrich. An **emu** runs fast, but it cannot fly.

envelope

An **envelope** is a flat paper container for a letter. You put a stamp on an **envelope** before you post a letter.

exercise

To **exercise** means to do a physical activity to keep fit. People **exercise** in many ways. Dean's favorite **exercise** is skipping.

eye

Your **eye** is the part of your body that you see with. You have two **eyes**.

Ff

face

Your **face** is the front of your head. A **face** has two eyes, a nose, two cheeks, a mouth, lips, and a chin.

factory

A **factory** is a large building where people make things. Ben's father works in a **factory** that makes engines.

fall

Fall is the season between summer and winter. In **fall** the leaves on many trees die and fall off.

family

A **family** is a group of people who are related to each other. Vivian's **family** includes her father, mother, brother, grandfather, and grandmother.

farm

A **farm** is an area of land where a farmer grows crops and keeps animals. The cows are eating grass in a field on the **farm**.

fast

To be **fast** means to be quick. **Fast** is the opposite of slow. Lauren is a **fast** runner.

fat

Fat means overweight or plump. The old cat is **fat** because it eats too much.

father

A **father** is a man who is a parent.

131

feather

A **feather** is a light, soft growth on the body of a bird. **Feathers** help a bird to fly.

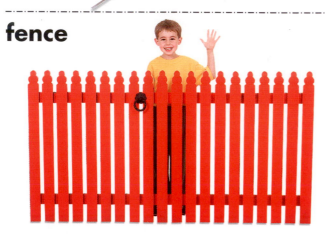

fence

A **fence** is a barrier that separates one area from another. **Fences** are made of wood, metal, or bricks.

film

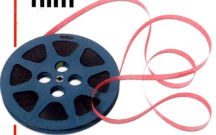

A **film** is a story told with moving pictures. **Films** are also called movies.

finger

Your **finger** is one of the slender parts at the end of your hand. People have four **fingers** and a thumb on each hand.

fire

A **fire** is the light, heat, and flames made when something burns.

fire engine

A **fire engine** is a vehicle that firefighters drive to a fire. A **fire engine** carries hoses to put out a fire.

first

To be **first** means to come in front of everything else. The red car came **first** in the race.

fish

A **fish** is an animal that lives in water. It has fins and a tail.

flag

A **flag** is a piece of material symbol. **Flags** are different colors and patterns. Each country has its own **flag**.

flamingo

A **flamingo** is a water bird with pink and scarlet feathers. A **flamingo** has very long legs and a long neck.

floor

A **floor** is the part of a room that people walk on. Alexandra is lying on the **floor**.

flower

A **flower** is part of a plant. Tammy picked some pretty **flowers** from the garden.

flute

A **flute** is a long, thin musical instrument. It is usually made of wood or metal. A **flute** is played with the mouth and fingers.

fly

To **fly** is to travel through the sky. Birds and beetles use their wings to **fly**. People **fly** in airplanes.

food

Food is what people and animals eat to stay alive.

foot

Your **foot** is the part of your body at the bottom of your legs. You have two **feet**.

forest

A **forest** is a place with lots of trees.

forget

To **forget** means not to remember. Did you **forget** to take your books to school today?

fork

A **fork** is a metal or plastic instrument that is used for eating. A **fork** has sharp prongs.

fox

A **fox** is a wild animal. It looks like small dog. A **fox** has a thick coat and tail.

friend

A **friend** is someone you like. **Friends** are fun to be with. Lachlan and Alexandra are best **friends**.

frog

A **frog** is a small animal that lives on land and in water. A **frog** has long back legs for jumping.

fruit

A **fruit** grows on a tree or bush. People and animals eat **fruit**.

full

To be **full** means to have no room for anything else. The case is **full** of buttons.

funny

To be **funny** means to make people laugh. When Talullah tells jokes, she is very **funny**.

fur

Fur is the soft, warm coat on an animal's body.

Gg

game

A **game** is something you play. **Games** have rules. Baseball and football are **games** played in a stadium. Some **games** are played on a board.

garden

A **garden** is a piece of land where grass, plants, or vegetables are grown.

gate

A **gate** is the part of a fence that opens and closes. Most **gates** are made of wood or steel.

giant

1. **Giant** means huge.
2. A **giant** is a huge person in a fairy tale.

giraffe

A **giraffe** is a tall animal with four long legs. A **giraffe** has a very long neck.

girl

A **girl** is a female child.
A **girl** grows into a woman.

135

give

To **give** means to hand something to someone. Lachlan is **giving** Charlotte a present.

glass

Glass is a hard material that is easy to break. **Glass** can be clear or colored.

glasses

Glasses are objects people wear to help them see. **Glasses** are also called spectacles. Alexandra wears **glasses**.

glove

A **glove** is a piece of clothing that covers a hand. People wear **gloves** to keep their hands warm.

glue

Glue is a liquid or paste used to stick things together. Josie uses **glue** to stick pictures in her scrapbook.

goat

A **goat** is an animal. It has four legs, a short tail, and horns. Some **goats** live on farms. Some **goats** are wild.

gold

Gold is a precious yellow metal found in rocks or riverbeds. It is often used to make jewelry.

goldfish

A **goldfish** is a small orange fish. It is often kept as a pet.

good

Good means well-behaved or nice. **Good** is the opposite of bad. Luke was a **good** boy because he helped his mother carry the shopping.

goose

A **goose** is a bird. It has strong wings, a long neck, and webbed feet.

grape

A **grape** is a fruit. **Grapes** grow in bunches on vines. People eat **grapes**. People also make wine from **grapes**.

grass

Grass is a plant with long thin leaves. Some animals eat **grass**.

grasshopper

A **grasshopper** is an insect. It has long back legs for jumping. Some **grasshoppers** make a chirping noise.

gray

Gray is a color. Sandra's grandmother has **gray** hair.

green

Green is a color. Grass is **green**.

group

A **group** is several people or things together. These blocks are in **groups** of three.

grow

To **grow** is to get bigger. A tree **grows**.

guitar

A **guitar** is a musical instrument. It is made of wood and has strings. A person plays the **guitar** by plucking the strings.

Hh

hair

Hair is what grows on your head. Charlotte wears her **hair** in a plait.

half

A **half** is one of two equal parts. This orange has been cut in **half**.

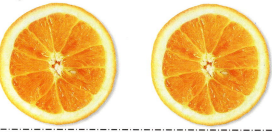

hamburger

A **hamburger** is a bun filled with **hamburger** meat and other foods, such as lettuce, tomato, and onion.

hammer

A **hammer** is a tool with a handle and a heavy metal head. A **hammer** is used to hit nails into wood.

hand

Your **hand** is the part of your body at the end of your arm. You have two **hands**. Your **hand** has a palm, four fingers, and a thumb.

happy

Happy means cheerful. **Happy** is the opposite of sad.

harbor

A **harbor** is a protected area of sea along a shore. Boats unload goods or passengers in a **harbor**.

hard

1. **Hard** means not soft. A rock is **hard**.
2. **Hard** means difficult. Schoolwork can be **hard**.

hat

A **hat** is a piece of clothing worn on the head.

hawk

A **hawk** is a bird with sharp claws and a curved beak. **Hawks** hunt small animals.

head

Your **head** is the part of your body above your neck. Your brain, skull, and face are all part of your **head**.

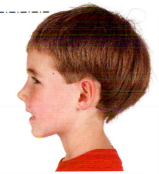

heart

Your **heart** is the muscle that beats in your chest. The **heart** is like a pump. It pumps blood around your body.

heavy

Heavy means weighing a lot. Lauren is carrying some **heavy** books.

helicopter

A **helicopter** is a flying machine. It has blades that spin instead of wings. A **helicopter** can fly, go up and down, and hover in the air.

helmet

A **helmet** is a hard hat that is worn to protect the head. A cyclist wears a **helmet**.

help

To **help** means to give aid or assistance. Alexandra **helps** her father wash the car.

hero

A **hero** is someone who does something very brave. Some **heroes** get medals.

hill

A **hill** is a piece of land that goes up, then down.

hip

Your **hip** is the part of your body that sticks out below your waist. Your legs are joined to your **hips**.

hippopotamus

A **hippopotamus** is a large African animal. A **hippopotamus** has short legs, a huge body, and a large mouth. A **hippopotamus** spends a lot of time in water.

hole

A **hole** is an opening through something. There is a **hole** in this sock.

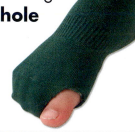

honey

Honey is a sweet, sticky liquid made by bees. **Honey** is a food. Some people like to eat **honey** spread on bread.

hook

A **hook** is a curved piece of metal or wood. People **hang** coats on hooks.

horse

A **horse** is a large animal with four legs, a mane, and a tail. People ride **horses**.

hospital

A **hospital** is a place where sick or injured people are looked after by doctors and nurses.

hot

Hot means very warm. Lachlan gets **hot** when he runs.

hour

An **hour** is a period of time. There are sixty minutes in one **hour**. There are twenty-four **hours** in one day.

house

A **house** is a building where people live.

hug

A **hug** is a warm, friendly squeeze with the arms. Alexandra **hugs** her teddy bear.

human

A **human** is a man, woman, or child. Every person is a **human**.

hungry

To be **hungry** is to want to eat. Jordan is **hungry** because he has not eaten since breakfast.

Ii

ice

Ice is water that has frozen solid.

ice cream

Ice cream is a frozen food made with milk, eggs, and sugar. Many people like to eat **ice cream** in a cone.

igloo

An **igloo** is a round house built from blocks of snow.

ink

Ink is a colored liquid. It is used for writing and for printing. Pens contain **ink**.

insect

An **insect** is a small animal with six legs. Some **insects** have wings. Butterflies, bees, and beetles are all **insects**.

inside

To be **inside** means to be in something. The jellybeans are **inside** the jar.

instrument

An **instrument** is an object that people play to make music. A trumpet is a musical **instrument**.

invite

To **invite** means to ask someone to come along or to visit you. Winona will **invite** all her friends to her birthday party.

Please come to my birthday party

iron

An **iron** is a tool that is heated and used to smooth creases from clothes.

island

An **island** is a piece of land that is surrounded by water.

itch

An **itch** is a feeling on your skin that makes you want to scratch that part of your body. Luke is scratching an **itch** on his arm.

ivy

Ivy is a climbing plant.

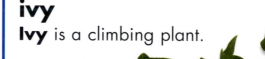

Jj

jacket

A **jacket** is a piece of clothing like a short coat. A **jacket** is worn on the upper body.

jaguar

A **jaguar** is a large wild cat. It has a spotted coat.

jar

A **jar** is a glass container used to hold things.

jaw

Your **jaw** is part of your head. It is the bone at the bottom of your skull. Your **jaw** moves up and down when you talk.

jelly

Jelly is a sweet food made from boiled fruit and sugar.

jet

A **jet** is an airplane that can fly very fast.

jewel

A **jewel** is a precious stone like a diamond or a ruby.

job

A **job** is the work a person does. Lachlan has a **job** delivering newspapers before school.

jockey

A **jockey** is a person who races horses.

joey

A **joey** is a baby kangaroo. A **joey** is carried in its mother's pouch.

joke

A **joke** is something somebody says or does to make people laugh. Dean has just heard a funny **joke**.

jug

A **jug** is a container with a handle and a spout. Liquids are kept in **jugs**. Melanie pours milk from a **jug** onto her breakfast cereal.

juice

Juice is the liquid part of a fruit. Alexandra drinks a glass of orange **juice** every morning.

jump

To **jump** is to leap into the air. Jordan can **jump** over his garden fence.

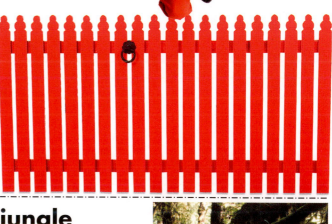

jungle

A **jungle** is a hot, tropical forest. Wild animals live in the **jungle**.

Kk

kangaroo

A **kangaroo** is an Australian animal. It has a long tail and strong back legs. **Kangaroos** move by jumping along the ground.

key

A **key** is an object that opens a lock. Most **keys** are made of metal. Helen used her **key** to unlock the front door.

kick

To **kick** is to hit something or someone with your foot. Luke **kicked** a ball into the air.

king

A **king** is a man who rules a country.

kiss

To **kiss** is to press your lips against someone as a greeting or sign of affection. Lauren **kissed** her mother on the cheek.

kitchen

A **kitchen** is a room in a house where meals are prepared and cooked.

kite

A **kite** is a light toy on a long string. You fly a **kite** in the sky.

kitten

A **kitten** is a young cat.

145

knee

Your **knee** is the middle part of your leg. Your leg bends at the **knee**.

knife

A **knife** is an object that is used for cutting. A **knife** has a sharp blade and a handle.

knock

To **knock** means to bang on or hit something. Luke is **knocking** on his friend's front door.

knot

A **knot** is a tie in one or more pieces of string, rope, or ribbon.

koala

A **koala** is an Australian animal. **Koalas** are furry. They live in trees and eat leaves.

Ll

ladder

A **ladder** is an object with wooden or metal steps. Charlotte stands on a **ladder** to paint the wall.

lake

A **lake** is a large area of water with land all around it.

lamb

A **lamb** is a young sheep.

lamp

A **lamp** is a light. Most **lamps** have a stand, a light bulb, a shade, and a switch.

large

Large means very big. A cargo ship is a **large** ship.

last

To be **last** is to come after everyone or everything else. Marian came **last** in the race. The letter Z comes **last** in the alphabet.

laugh

To **laugh** means to make a sound that shows amusement. People **laugh** at something funny.

leaf

A **leaf** is a part of a plant.

leg

Your **leg** is the part of your body that you use to walk. You have two **legs**. Some animals have four **legs**. Insects have six **legs**.

lemon

A **lemon** is a sour, tangy fruit. **Lemons** are yellow.

letter

1. A **letter** is a written message that is sent to someone. 2. A **letter** is one of the parts of the alphabet, such as A, B, and C. **Letters** are used to make words.

lettuce

A **lettuce** is a vegetable. It has big green leaves. **Lettuce** is often eaten in a salad.

library

A **library** is a building where books are kept on shelves. People can borrow books from a **library**.

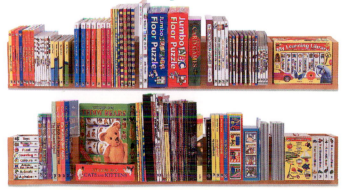

147

lighthouse

A **lighthouse** is a tall building on the coast. It has a flashing light at the top. People on ships see the light and know not to bring their ship too close to the shore.

lion

A **lion** is a powerful wild animal. **Lions** belong to the cat family. They live in Africa and India. A male **lion** has a mane. A female **lion** is called a lioness.

lightning

Lightning is a flash of light in the sky during a thunderstorm.

lip

Your **lip** is one of the fleshy parts around your mouth. You have two **lips**. People kiss each other with their **lips**.

little

Little means small. Babies are **little**.

limb

A **limb** is a leg or an arm. People have four **limbs**. Your **limbs** are your two legs and your two arms.

lizard

A **lizard** is an animal with scaly skin and four legs. Most **lizards** lay eggs.

lobster

A **lobster** is a sea animal. It has a shell and ten legs. There are two big claws on the first pair of legs.

lock

A **lock** is an object that is used to keep something shut. A key is needed to open a **lock**.

log

A **log** is a piece of wood that has been cut from a tree.

lollipop

A **lollipop** is a piece of hard candy on a stick.

long

Long is the opposite of short. An elephant has a **long** trunk.

look

To **look** means to use your eyes to see something. Lauren is **looking** at herself in a mirror.

love

To **love** means to like a person or something very much. Charlotte **loves** her mother.

lunch

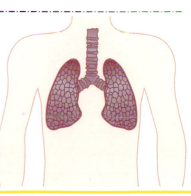

Lunch is a meal that people eat in the middle of the day.

lung

Your **lung** is the part of your body that you breathe with. You have two **lungs** inside your chest.

Mm

machine

A **machine** is an object that has moving parts. A **machine** does work for people. The engine in a car is a **machine**.

magnet

A **magnet** is a piece of iron or steel that pulls other pieces of metal to it.

magnify

To **magnify** something is to make it look bigger.

mammal

A **mammal** is an animal that drinks its mother's milk when it is young. People, dogs, and rabbits are all **mammals**.

man

A **man** is an adult male person. Boys become **men**.

map

A **map** is a drawing that shows where places are. A **map** can show countries. A **map** can show streets.

marble

A **marble** is a small glass ball. It is a toy. Children play games with **marbles**.

mask

A **mask** is a covering for the face. People often wear **masks** for fun. Zoran is painting a **mask** on Gemma's face.

meat

Meat is the flesh of animals. **Meat** is eaten as food.

medicine

Medicine is what sick people take to get better. Mel had a bad cough, so he took some cough **medicine**.

mermaid

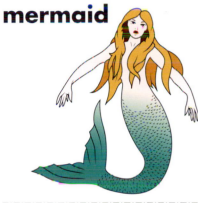

A **mermaid** is an imaginary creature. A **mermaid** is half woman and half fish.

merry-go-round

A **merry-go-round** is a machine in an amusement park or fairground that people ride on for fun. A **merry-go-round** goes round and round.

metal

Metal is a hard substance that is used to make tools and other objects. Iron, steel, gold, and silver are all **metals**.

microscope

A **microscope** is an instrument that makes tiny things look bigger. A person looks through a **microscope**.

microwave

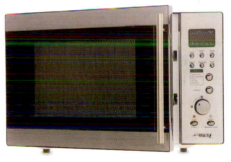

A **microwave** oven cooks food very quickly with electric waves.

middle

The **middle** is the center of something. The vase is in the **middle** of the table.

milk

Milk is a white liquid made by some animals. People drink **milk**. A baby drinks its mother's **milk**.

minute

A **minute** is a period of time. There are sixty seconds in one **minute**. There are sixty **minutes** in one hour.

mirror

A **mirror** is a special piece of glass in which you can see yourself. Tara looks in the **mirror** when she combs her hair.

money

Money is what people use to buy things. Coins and bank notes are **money**.

monkey

A **monkey** is a furry animal with long arms and strong hands. Most **monkeys** have a long tail and live in trees.

monster

A **monster** is a huge, terrifying creature. There are **monsters** in some fairy tales.

month

A **month** lasts about thirty days. There are twelve **months** in one year.

January February March
April May June
July August September
October November December

moon

The **moon** is a large, bright object in the sky. The **moon** can often be seen at night. The **moon** goes around the earth once every month.

morning

The **morning** is the time of the day that follows the night.

mother

A **mother** is a woman who is a parent.

mountain

A **mountain** is a large area of raised land. The sides of **mountains** are often steep.

mouse

A **mouse** is a tiny animal that has sharp teeth and a long tail.

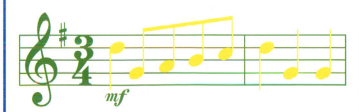

mouth

Your **mouth** is the opening in your face beneath your nose. You use your **mouth** for eating, breathing, and speaking.

mug

A **mug** is a large drinking cup with a handle.

muscle

A **muscle** is a part of your body. You have many **muscles**. The **muscles** in Lauren's arms help her lift heavy things.

mushroom

A **mushroom** is a plant that looks like a little umbrella. Some **mushrooms** are good to eat. A **mushroom** is also called a fungus.

music

Music is a group of sounds. **Music** is made by voices and by instruments.

Nn

nail

A **nail** is a thick, sharp, metal pin with a flat top.

naked

Naked means not wearing any clothes.

neck

Your **neck** is the narrow part of your body between your head and your shoulders.

necklace

A **necklace** is a piece of jewelry that is worn around the neck.

needle

A **needle** is a thin, sharp piece of steel with a hole at one end. A **needle** is used for sewing.

nest

A **nest** is the place where a bird lays its eggs. Baby birds live in **nests**.

new

New means just made. Caleb bought some **new** shoes.

newspaper

A **newspaper** contains stories and photographs. People read **newspapers** to learn about events that have just happened.

night

Night is the time of the day between sunset and sunrise. It is dark at **night**.

noise

A **noise** is a sound. Some **noises** are very loud. Lachlan makes a loud **noise** when he bangs his drum.

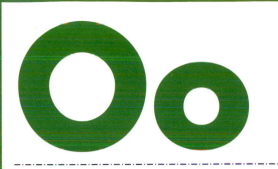

nose

Your **nose** is the part of your body between your eyes and mouth. You smell and breathe through your **nose**.

number

A **number** is a figure that is used in counting. One, two, three, four, five, six, seven, eight, nine, and ten are all **numbers**.

nurse

A **nurse** is a person who looks after sick or injured people. Many **nurses** wear uniforms and work in hospitals.

nut

A **nut** is a dry fruit inside a hard shell.

Oo

ocean

An **ocean** is a very large area of salt water. The largest **ocean** in the world is the Pacific Ocean.

office

An **office** is a place where people work. Dale's father works in an **office** at home. Dale's mother works in an **office** in the city.

old

To be **old** means to have been made or born a long time ago. Hermione loves her **old** teddy bear.

onion

An **onion** is a vegetable with a sharp smell and taste. The smell of an **onion** can bring tears to a person's eyes.

open

Open means not shut. The box is **open**.

orange

An **orange** is a round, juicy fruit.

orchard

An **orchard** is a field where fruit trees grow. Apple trees grow in an **orchard**.

orchestra

An **orchestra** is a large group of people who play musical instruments together. Violins, drums, trumpets, flutes, and other instruments are played by the musicians in an **orchestra**.

origami

Origami is a way of folding paper to make interesting shapes.

ostrich

An **ostrich** is a large bird with long legs and huge feathers. An **ostrich** cannot fly. It can run very fast.

otter

An **otter** is a small, furry water animal. It has webbed feet and a long flat tail.

oval

An **oval** is a shape like an egg. Some footballs are **oval**-shaped.

oven

An **oven** is an electric or gas machine that is used for cooking food.

owl

An **owl** is a bird with big eyes, soft feathers, and fierce claws. Most **owls** hunt at night.

oyster

An **oyster** is a shellfish. It has a hard shell and a soft body.

Pp

pain

Pain is a feeling that hurts. Charlotte ate a whole box of chocolates. Now she has a **pain** in her stomach.

paint

Paint is a colored liquid. **Paint** is used on walls and to make pictures.

pajamas

Pajamas are the loose clothes people wear in bed.

palm

Your **palm** is the inside part of your hand. Gabrielle is holding a shell in the **palm** of her hand.

panda

A **panda** is a large animal that looks like a bear. **Pandas** are black and white. They live in China.

paper

Paper is a material that people write, print, or draw on. Books, magazines, cards, and newspapers are made of **paper**.

parachute

A **parachute** is a piece of material shaped like an umbrella. It has straps and cords.

parcel

A **parcel** is an object wrapped in paper.

park

A **park** is a place where people go to walk and play. Most **parks** have trees, grass, paths, and a playground.

parrot

A **parrot** is a colorful bird with a curved beak. Pet **parrots** can often be taught to speak a few words.

party

A **party** is a group of friends who meet to have fun together.

paw

A **paw** is the foot of an animal. The cat is licking its **paw**.

pea

A **pea** is a small, round vegetable. **Peas** grow inside pods.

peach

A **peach** is a juicy fruit with a hard stone in the middle.

peanut

A **peanut** is a small nut that grows in the ground.

pear

A **pear** is a sweet fruit that grows on trees.

pearl

A **pearl** is a jewel. **Pearls** grow in some oysters. This is a **pearl** necklace.

pelican

A **pelican** is a water bird. Its big beak has a pouch for holding the fish it catches.

pen

A **pen** is a tool people write or draw with. A **pen** is long and thin. It is filled with ink.

pencil

A **pencil** is a tool people write or draw with. A **pencil** is a thin piece of wood with a stick of lead in the middle.

penguin

A **penguin** is a bird that lives in very cold places. A **penguin** can swim. It cannot fly.

pet

A **pet** is a tame animal that a person looks after at home. Talullah has a **pet** rabbit.

photograph

A **photograph** is a picture that is taken by a machine called a camera.

piano

A **piano** is a musical instrument.

picnic

A **picnic** is a meal that is eaten in the open air. Alexandra and her friends are having a **picnic**.

pig

A **pig** is a farm animal. It has short legs and a flat nose.

pigeon

A **pigeon** is a fast-flying bird. Most **pigeons** are gray. Some people keep **pigeons** as pets.

pilot

A **pilot** is a person who flies an airplane.

pineapple

A **pineapple** is a large fruit with a thick, rough skin.

pink

Pink is a pale red color. Strawberry ice cream is **pink**.

pirate

A **pirate** is a person who robs ships at sea.

planet

A **planet** is an object in space that moves around a star. **Planets** are big and round. Earth is a **planet**. So are Mercury, Venus, Mars, Jupiter, Saturn, Uranus, Neptune, and Pluto.

plant

A **plant** is something that grows in the ground. **Plants** are alive. Many **plants** have green leaves, a stem, and roots.

plate

A **plate** is a flat dish. Most plates are round. Food is served on a **plate**.

playground

A **playground** is a place where children play on equipment, such as swings and see-saws.

pocket

A **pocket** is a small cloth pouch sewn into clothing. Dean's **pockets** are empty.

poison

Poison is a liquid or substance that can kill or harm you if it gets into your body.

police

The **police** are people who make sure people obey the law. The **police** protect people and property. The **police** put criminals in jail.

pond

A **pond** is a small area of water. Water lilies are growing in this **pond**.

pony

A **pony** is a small horse.

porcupine

A **porcupine** is an animal. It is covered with long, sharp spines.

potato

A **potato** is a small vegetable that grows in the ground.

pregnant

Pregnant means having a baby growing inside. This woman is **pregnant**. The baby is due next month.

present

A **present** is a gift. Molly gave her sister a birthday **present**.

pretend

To **pretend** is to make believe. Dean is **pretending** to be a spider.

price

The **price** is the amount of money a person pays for something.

prize

A **prize** is a reward. Jeremiah and his cat won first **prize** at the cat show.

pull

To **pull** is to drag or tug something toward you. Luke is **pulling** on a rope.

pump

A **pump** is a machine that pushes air or liquid in or out of an object. A bicycle **pump** pushes air into the tires.

pumpkin

A **pumpkin** is a large, orange fruit.

puppet

A **puppet** is a doll that can move. A hand **puppet** fits over a person's hand. This **puppet** has strings. The **puppet** moves when the strings are pulled.

puppy

A **puppy** is a young dog.

purple

Purple is a color.

push

To **push** is to press or shove something away from you. Lauren is **pushing** Dean on his tricycle.

puzzle

A **puzzle** is a question, a game, or a mystery. People try to find the answer to a **puzzle**.

python

A **python** is a big snake. A **python** wraps itself around its prey.

Qq

quarter

A **quarter** is one of four equal parts.

queen

A **queen** is a woman who rules a country.

question

A **question** is what you ask when you want information. Jordan asked his teacher a **question** about his homework.

queue

A **queue** is a line of people waiting in turn. There was a long **queue** at the bus stop.

quiet

Quiet means to make very little noise. Jordan told his sister to be **quiet**.

quilt

A **quilt** is a warm cover for a bed. Most **quilts** are filled with feathers.

quiz

A **quiz** is a game. One person asks another person or a group of people questions to find out what they know.

Rr

rabbit

A **rabbit** is a furry animal with a tiny tail and large ears. **Rabbits** live in holes in the ground called burrows.

race

A **race** is a test to see who or what is the fastest. Lachlan and Charlotte are having a sack **race**.

radio

A **radio** is a machine that receives electrical signals sent through the air. A person can listen to music, talk shows, and other programs on a **radio**.

rain

Rain is water that falls from clouds. **Rain** falls in drops.

rake

A **rake** is a garden tool. It has a long handle and long teeth.

rat

A **rat** is an animal. It looks like a large mouse. It has a long tail, whiskers, and sharp teeth.

rattle

A **rattle** is an object that makes a noise when it is shaken. Babies play with **rattles**.

reach

To **reach** means to stretch out a hand to touch something.

read

To **read** means to look at and understand words. What sort of books do you like to **read**?

receive

To **receive** is to get something from someone.

recipe

A **recipe** is a set of instructions that tell you how to cook something.

rectangle

A **rectangle** is a shape with four sides. Two sides of a **rectangle** are longer than the other two sides.

recycle

To **recycle** means to use something again. Bottles and jars can be **recycled**.

red

Red is a color. A tomato is **red**.

refrigerator

A **refrigerator** is a large container for keeping food and drink cold and fresh.

relax

To **relax** is to feel calm and comfortable. Jordan **relaxes** by reading a book.

reptile

A **reptile** is a cold-blooded animal with a backbone. Crocodiles, lizards, and snakes are all **reptiles**.

restaurant

A **restaurant** is a place where you buy and eat a meal.

rhinoceros

A **rhinoceros** is a large, heavy animal. It has one or two horns on its nose.

ribbon

A **ribbon** is a strip of colored material.

rice

Rice is a food. Grains of **rice** can be boiled or fried.

ride

To **ride** is to sit and travel in a vehicle or on an animal.

ring

A **ring** is a piece of jewelry. Irene wears a ring on her finger.

river

A **river** is a wide stream of fresh water.

road

A **road** is a hard, wide path that cars, trucks, and other vehicles travel on.

robot

A **robot** is a machine that does a set job. Some robots are used in factories. This is a toy **robot**.

rock

A **rock** is a large stone.

rocket

A **rocket** is a machine that shoots into space. A **rocket** takes off from a launching pad.

roof

A **roof** is the top part of a building. A **roof** keeps the sun and rain out.

rope

A **rope** is a thick piece of string or cord.

rose

A **rose** is a pretty flower. Some **roses** have a sweet smell.

round

Round means shaped like a ball or circle.

rubber

Rubber is a strong material that stretches. Car tires are made of **rubber**.

rug

A **rug** is a small carpet. **Rugs** come in many different colors and shapes.

ruler

A **ruler** is a flat, straight piece of wood or metal. People use **rulers** to draw straight lines and to measure things.

run

To **run** is to move quickly using your legs.

Ss

sad

To be **sad** is to be unhappy. Jordan is **sad** because his goldfish died. **Sad** is the opposite of happy.

saddle

A **saddle** is a leather seat that fits on the back of a horse.

sail

A **sail** on a boat is a large piece of material that catches the wind.

salad

A **salad** is a dish of raw vegetables.

sand

Sand is made of tiny grains of rock. A beach is made of **sand**.

sandwich

A **sandwich** is two pieces of bread with a filling between them.

scarecrow

A **scarecrow** is a figure dressed in old clothes. A farmer puts a **scarecrow** in a field to scare birds away from the crops.

scared

To be **scared** is to be frightened.

scarf

A **scarf** is a piece of warm clothing. A **scarf** is worn wrapped around the neck or head.

school

A **school** is a place where people learn new skills. Teachers work in **schools**.

scientist

A **scientist** is a person whose job it is to find answers to questions about science topics. **Scientists** do experiments.

scissors

Scissors are a tool used for cutting. **Scissors** have two long blades.

scream

To **scream** means to cry out loudly.

sea

A **sea** is a large area of salt water.

seal

A **seal** is a sea animal with a long, sleek body and flippers.

secret

A **secret** is information that people keep to themselves. Jordan did not tell Annie that he had bought her a present. He kept it a **secret**.

see

To **see** is to look at things. People use their eyes to **see**.

seed

A **seed** is a tiny part of a plant. **Seeds** grow into new plants.

sell

To **sell** is to swap something for money. Lachlan **sold** his comic book to Alexandra.

shadow

A **shadow** is a dark shape surrounded by light. Helen stood before a light and made **shadow** puppets on the wall.

shampoo

Shampoo is a liquid soap for washing hair.

share

To **share** is to use something together. Lauren **shared** her toys with Dean.

shark

A **shark** is a large fish. It has very sharp teeth.

sheep

A **sheep** is a farm animal with a thick woolly coat.

shell

A **shell** is a hard covering. Nuts and eggs have **shells**. Animals like turtles and shellfish have **shells**.

ship

A **ship** is a large boat.

shirt

A **shirt** is a piece of clothing that is worn on the upper body.

shoe

A **shoe** is a covering for a foot. **Shoes** are sold in pairs.

short

Short means not long. Luke has **short** hair.

shoulder

Your **shoulder** is the part of your body below your neck. Your arms are joined to your **shoulders**.

sing

To **sing** is to make musical sounds with the voice. Dean is **singing** into a microphone.

sister

A **sister** is a girl or woman who has the same parents as another person. Leah and Annemarie are **sisters**. They have the same father and mother.

size

Size is how big or small something is. What **size** shoe do you take?

skate

A **skate** is a special shoe with a sharp metal blade or wheels on the bottom.

skateboard

A **skateboard** is a board on wheels that a person rides on for fun.

skeleton

Your **skeleton** is the framework of bones that supports your body.

ski

To **ski** means to travel over snow on **skis**. People wear **skis** on their feet.

skin

Skin is what covers a person or animal. Some plants also have **skins**.

skirt

A **skirt** is a piece of clothing that hangs from the waist. **Skirts** can be different lengths.

sky

The **sky** is the upper air and the part of outer space that can be seen from earth. The **sky** is usually blue during the day.

skyscraper

A **skyscraper** is a very tall office or apartment building. It is called a **skyscraper** because it looks as if it is touching the sky.

sled

A **sled** is a vehicle on runners for traveling over snow. A **sled** carries people and objects.

sleep

To **sleep** is to rest deeply with your eyes shut. Most people **sleep** at night.

slow

Slow means to move or act with little speed. Turtles are **slow**.

small

Small means not big. The **small** ball is on the left.

smell

A **smell** is a scent or odor that your nose can detect.

smile

A **smile** is a happy look made by turning the corners of the mouth up.

snail

A **snail** is a small animal that has a shell on its back. A **snail** travels very slowly.

snake

A **snake** is an animal with a long body and no legs.

snow

Snow is flakes of frozen water falling from the sky.

snowman

A **snowman** is a person made from snow.

soap

Soap is a bar, powder or liquid. People use **soap** with water to wash themselves or things.

sock

A **sock** is a piece of clothing worn on a foot. **Socks** are worn under shoes.

soft

Soft means nice and gentle to touch. A kitten's fur is **soft**.

song

A **song** is what a person sings. A **song** has words and music.

space

Space is the area beyond earth. It is also called outer **space**.

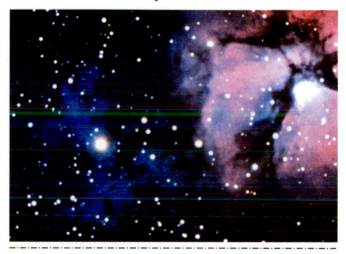

spacecraft

A **spacecraft** is a machine that travels in space.

spade

A **spade** is a tool with a long handle and a metal blade.

spell

To **spell** is to speak or write the letters of a word in the correct order.

C-A-T spells cat

spider

A **spider** is an animal with eight legs. Most **spiders** spin webs to catch insects to eat.

spin

To **spin** is to turn yourself or something around very quickly.

spoon

A **spoon** is a metal or plastic instrument that is used for eating food.
A **spoon** has a handle and one round or oval end.

sport

Sport is a game. People often play **sport** in teams. Baseball, football, tennis, and cricket are all **sports**.

spring

Spring is the season between winter and summer. Flowers grow in **spring**.

square

A **square** is a shape.
A **square** has four sides of the same length.

squash

To **squash** means to press something until it is flat.

squeeze

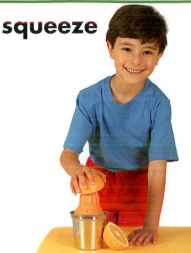

To **squeeze** is to press on all sides. Dean is **squeezing** an orange to get the juice.

squirrel

A **squirrel** is an animal with a bushy tail. **Squirrels** live in trees.

stairs

Stairs are a set of steps. People go up and down **stairs**.

stamp

A **stamp** is a tiny piece of paper that a person sticks on an envelope.

stand

To **stand** means to be upright on your feet.

star

A **star** is a bright object in the sky that looks like a shining dot. **Stars** can usually be seen in the sky at night.

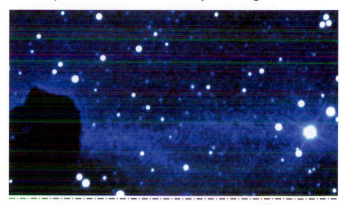

starfish

A **starfish** is a sea animal that has lots of arms. A **starfish** looks like a star.

statue

A **statue** is a model of a person or animal. **Statues** are usually made from rock, wood, or metal.

stomach

Your **stomach** is the part of your body that stores and digests the food you eat.

store

A **store** is a place where people buy things.

storm

A **storm** is wild weather. There is often rain, strong winds, lightning and thunder during a **storm**.

strawberry

A **strawberry** is a juicy red fruit.

string

String is thin cord used for tying things.

submarine

A **submarine** is a ship that travels beneath the sea.

summer

Summer is the hottest season of the year. It comes between spring and fall. People wear cool clothes in **summer**.

sun

The **sun** is the brightest object in the sky during the day. The **sun** warms the earth. The **sun** is a star.

swan

A **swan** is a large water bird with a long neck. Most **swans** have white feathers and black feet.

swim

To **swim** is to move through the water using your arms and legs. Dean **swims** ten laps of the pool every morning.

Tt

table

A **table** is a piece of furniture with a flat top and legs.

tail

A **tail** is the bottom end of some animals. A dog wags its **tail** when it is happy.

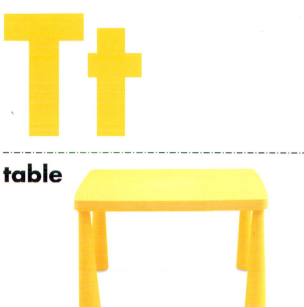

tale

A **tale** is a story. The teacher told the class a **tale** about a giant and a magic seed.

talk

To **talk** means to speak. Talullah and Dean are **talking**.

tanker

A **tanker** is a truck or ship that carries liquids or gases.

target

A **target** is an object you aim at. Peter threw a dart at the **target**.

teacher

A **teacher** is a person who teaches other people. Many **teachers** work in schools.

team

A **team** is a group of people who play or work together. These children play for the same basketball **team**.

teeth

Your **teeth** are the small hard pieces inside your mouth. **Teeth** are used for biting and chewing food.

telephone

A **telephone** is a machine that a person uses to speak with another person who is far away.

television

A **television** is a machine that receives and shows moving pictures and sounds.

tennis

Tennis is a sport played by two or four people on a court. Each player uses a racket to hit the ball over a net.

tent

A **tent** is a shelter. A **tent** is made of cloth and held up by poles and ropes. Luke sleeps in a **tent** when he goes camping.

thermometer

A **thermometer** is an instrument for measuring temperature. The nurse put a **thermometer** in the patient's mouth to take his temperature.

throat

Your **throat** is the passage at the back of your mouth. Food, drink and air go down tubes inside your **throat**.

thumb

Your **thumb** is the thick, short finger on your hand. You have two **thumbs**.

tiger

A **tiger** is a large wild animal. Its fur is orange with black stripes. The **tiger** is a member of the cat family.

toe

Your **toe** is one of the digits on your foot. You have five **toes** on each foot.

tomato

A **tomato** is a round red fruit.

tongue

Your **tongue** is the soft, movable muscle inside your mouth.

tool

A **tool** is an instrument that helps a person do a job. Hammers, screwdrivers, and saws are all **tools**.

toothbrush

A **toothbrush** is a small brush that is used for cleaning teeth.

top

Top means the highest place or part. Lachlan is at the **top** of the slide.

towel

A **towel** is a large piece of cloth. People use **towels** to dry themselves.

town

A **town** is a place where lots of people live and work. A **town** is bigger than a village, but smaller than a city.

toy

A **toy** is an object that children play with. This train is a **toy**.

tractor

A **tractor** is a large vehicle used on a farm. A **tractor** can pull heavy plows and trailers.

traffic

Traffic is moving vehicles.

tree

A **tree** is a large plant. Most **trees** have a trunk, branches, and leaves.

triangle

A **triangle** is a shape with three straight sides.

trousers

Trousers are a piece of clothing. **Trousers** cover the legs.

truck

A **truck** is a large vehicle with wheels. **Trucks** carry things.

T-shirt

A **T-shirt** is a piece of clothing that is worn on the upper body. A **T-shirt** has short sleeves. It is called a **T-shirt** because it is made in the shape of a letter T.

tunnel

A **tunnel** is a passage that goes underground or through something.

turkey

A **turkey** is a big bird. Some **turkeys** are raised on farms for their meat.

turn

1. To **turn** is to change direction.
2. A **turn** is a bend in a place like a road or track.

turtle

A **turtle** is an animal with a hard shell on its back. A **turtle** can pull its legs and head inside its shell.

twins

Twins are two babies born at the same time to the same mother. Identical **twins** look alike.

Uu

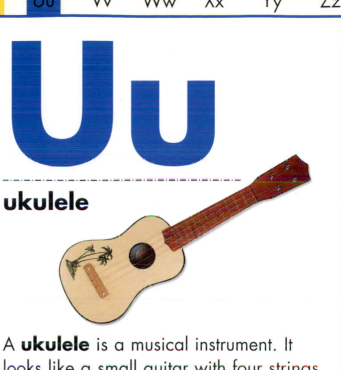

ukulele

A **ukulele** is a musical instrument. It looks like a small guitar with four strings.

umbrella

An **umbrella** is an object that protects people from the rain. It has a long handle and the top is made of cloth.

under

Under means to be beneath something. The puppy is **under** the blanket.

unhappy

To be **unhappy** means to be sad. The opposite of **unhappy** is happy.

unicorn

A **unicorn** is a make-believe animal. It looks like a horse with a horn on its head.

up

Up means to a higher place. The hot-air balloon went **up** into the sky.

Vv

vase

A **vase** is an object for holding cut flowers.

vegetable

A **vegetable** is a part of a plant. People eat **vegetables**.

vehicle

A **vehicle** is a machine that transports people and goods. A car is a **vehicle**.

vet

A **vet** is a doctor who looks after sick animals. **Vet** is short for veterinary surgeon.

videotape

Videotape is the tape that is used in a video camera to record pictures and sounds.

village

A **village** is a small place in the country where people live. A **village** usually has a few shops.

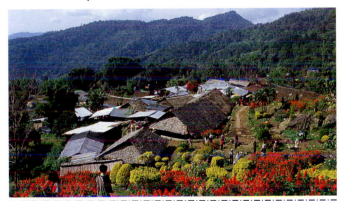

violin

A **violin** is a musical instrument. It has four strings. A person plays a **violin** by rubbing a stick called a bow across the strings.

voice

Your **voice** is the sound you make when you talk or sing.

volcano

A **volcano** is a mountain with a hole in the top. Sometimes hot rock, gas, and ash come out of a **volcano**.

vulture

A **vulture** is a large bird. **Vultures** feed on dead animals.

Ww

wagon

A **wagon** is a vehicle with four wheels. **Wagons** carry heavy loads. They are often pulled by horses or oxen.

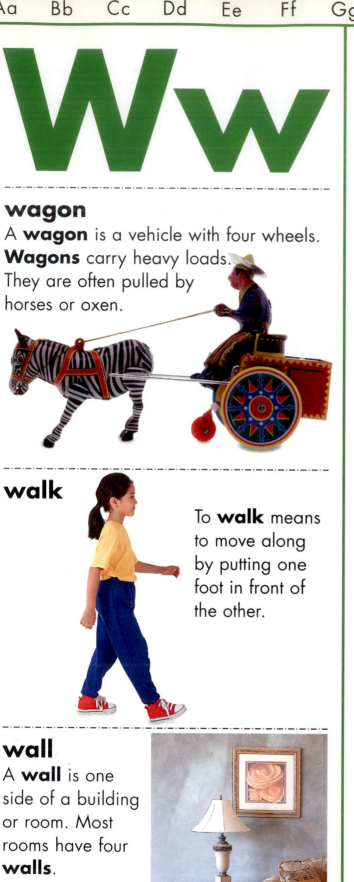

walk

To **walk** means to move along by putting one foot in front of the other.

wall

A **wall** is one side of a building or room. Most rooms have four **walls**.

walnut

A **walnut** is a tasty nut in a hard shell. **Walnuts** grow on trees.

walrus

A **walrus** is a large sea animal. A **walrus** has flippers and two long tusks.

wash

To **wash** means to clean something with soap and water. Alexandra **washed** her face.

watch

A **watch** is a small clock that is worn on the wrist.

water

Water is a clear liquid that people, animals, and plants drink.

waterproof

Waterproof means able to keep water out. Luke wears a **waterproof** coat when it rains.

wave

1. To **wave** is to move your hand in the air. People **wave** as a way of saying hello or goodbye. 2. A **wave** is a curling sheet of water moving on the surface of the sea.

weather

The **weather** is what it is like outside. What is the **weather** like today? Is it sunny, windy, or stormy?

week

A **week** is a period of time. There are seven days in one **week**.

Sunday   Monday   Tuesday   Wednesday   Thursday   Friday   Saturday

weigh

To **weigh** means to measure how heavy someone or something is.

wet

Wet means to be damp or covered with water. Dean has **wet** hair.

whale

A **whale** is a large sea animal. A **whale** has a large body, flippers, and a tail. **Whales** breathe through blowholes on the top of their heads.

wheel

A **wheel** is a round object that turns. A car moves on its **wheels**.

whisper

To **whisper** means to speak very quietly. Luke **whispered** a secret to Lauren.

whistle

A **whistle** is an instrument that makes a shrill noise when a person blows into it.

white

White is a very pale color. Snow is **white**.

wind

The **wind** is moving air. The **wind** blew leaves into the air.

windmill

A **windmill** is a machine with sails or blades. The wind turns the sails or blades. A **windmill** can be used to grind grain, pump water, or to make electricity.

window

A **window** is a glass surface that a person can look out of.

wing

A **wing** is a part of a bird or an airplane.

winter

Winter is the coldest season of the year. **Winter** is between fall and spring. People wear warm clothes in **winter**.

wire

Wire is a metal thread. Electricity can flow through a **wire**.

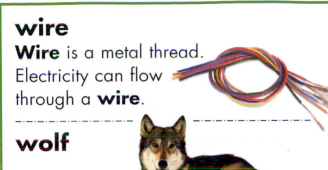

wolf

A **wolf** is a wild animal. It looks like a dog. **Wolves** live in groups called packs.

woman

A **woman** is an adult female person. Girls become **women**.

wool

Wool grows on sheep. **Wool** is a soft, warm material.

work

To **work** means to do a job to earn money.

world

The **world** is the planet Earth.

worm

A **worm** is a long, thin animal. It has a soft body and no legs. **Worms** live in tiny tunnels under the ground.

wrist

Your **wrist** is the part of your body that joins your hand to your arm.

write

To **write** is to make letters, words, or numbers with a pen or pencil. You can **write** on a piece of paper or on a blackboard.

Xx

X-ray

An **X-ray** is a special photograph of the inside of your body.

xylophone

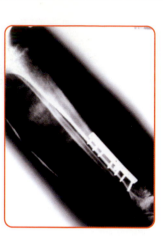

A **xylophone** is a musical instrument. It is made of a row of wooden or metal bars. The bars are different lengths. When a person hits the bars with soft hammers, the bars make different sounds.

Yy

yacht

A **yacht** is a boat with sails.

yawn

To **yawn** is to take a deep breath with your mouth open wide. You **yawn** when you are tired or bored.

year

A **year** is a period of time. There are twelve months in one **year**.

yell

To **yell** means to shout or cry out. Lachlan **yelled** when his football team scored a goal.

190

yellow
Yellow is a bright color. Bananas are **yellow**.

yogurt
Yogurt is a thick creamy food made from milk.

yolk
A **yolk** is the yellow part of an egg.

young
Young means not old. A **young** animal or plant has not been alive for very long.

yo-yo
A **yo-yo** is a plastic or wooden toy. A person loops the string around a finger and makes the **yo-yo** spin up and down on the string.

Zz

zebra

A **zebra** is a wild animal. It looks like a horse. A **zebra** has black and white stripes on its body.

zip
A **zip** is a fastener that holds a piece of clothing together.

zoo
A **zoo** is a place where animals are kept in enclosures for people to look at.

191

HINKLER
BOOKS

Published in 2005 by Hinkler Books Pty Ltd
17–23 Redwood Drive
Dingley VIC 3172
Australia
www.hinklerbooks.com

ISBN 1 7415 7029 8

© Hinkler Books Pty Ltd 2005

10 9 8 7 6 5 4
10 09 08 07

First 1000 Words:
Written by Julie Haydon
Designed by Ivan Finnegan

First Picture Dictionary:
Written by Archie Oliver
Edited by Julie Haydon
Designed by Andrew Burgess

Photography by Peter Wakeman

Models: Laurie Bicknell, Jordan Boak, Andrew Burgess, Georgina Delbridge, Charlotte Delbridge,
Jacob Delbridge, Andrew Delbridge, Damien Dennis, Tricia Dennis, Gabriel Finnegan, Luke Gorrie, Jake Gregory,
Jennifer Hall, Dean Koumantaros, Joannne Lloyd, Alexandra and Charlotte McCristal, Tony McGrath, Gitte Mortensen,
Talullah-Lili Lloyd Murray, Ibo Owner, Chris Pakes, Lachlan Raverty, Lauren Retica, David Ricardo, Sam Ricardo,
Charlotte Thompson, Wendy Ungar.

Airport photograph reproduced with the kind permission of Melbourne Airport.

Cover Design: Hoyne Design

Printed and bound in China